Y0-BGE-887

The Amish Family

by *Norma Fischer Furey*

Illustrations By: Pam Goller

Cover Photo By: Doyle Yoder

© *1996 - New Horizons Publishing Company*

All rights reserved. Reproduction or translation of any part of this publication without the express written consent of the publisher is prohibited. Requests for permission or further information should be addressed to:

New Horizons Publishing
P.O. Box 226
New Wilmington, PA 16142
ISBN 1-884687-03-2
Library of Congress Catalog Card Number 96-069842
Printed and bound in the United States of America by Globe Graphics &
Printing Company, New Wilmington, PA 16142.

DEDICATION

To my beloved Eddy Joe ...
"...Thank God for you...you are the wind beneath my wings..."

Norma Fischer Furey

About The Author

Norma Fischer Fuery was born in Pittsburgh, but at the age of 2 1/2 the family moved to rural Mercer County, Pennsylvania, where she was raised among the Old Order Amish, and became friends with several Amish families. Her father was fluent in German and conversed easily with their Amish friends. The Amish children, especially, were always surprised, but delighted, to have an "English" (as used to refer to the non-Amish) who spoke their language. Norma holds a Bachelor's Degree in library science from Edinboro University of Pennsylvania, and a Master's of Library and Information Science from the University of Pittsburgh. While working as a school librarian in Pennsylvania's Cumberland Valley, she also studied at Shippensburg University of Pennsylvania. Although her credentials enable her to work in libraries at all levels, she has chosen to be a high school librarian. Norma believes that high school students must be taught how to do research, and how to use the hundreds of reference books, documents and CD/ROM sources available before they are in college, or on the job. "There is a challenge each time there is a fact to look up or a term paper to be written. It becomes like a treasure hunt and the reward is the information discovered during the search!" She has worked in public libraries, as well, and especially enjoys the challenge of genealogical research. "The excitement of discovering one's past is unequalled and is possible, in large part, because of the thousands of documents that have been preserved and/or placed on microforms. The priceless chronicles and records of families must always be regarded as treasures to be cherished and preserved and made available for future generations. Much of the research for this book could not have been done without the carefully maintained and cataloged records of the Amish people. This very important archival material might well have been lost without the modern preservation methods and caring individuals who recognized the need to make the information available to the public."

The works of John A. Hostetler has been invaluable. His scholarly approach, personal experiences and obvious appreciation of the Amish way of life provided a rich background for the research required to complete this work. The Amish deserve our respect and every effort has been made in this work to avoid the exploitation of her personal friends, as well as all of the reverent, hard-working followers of Jakob Amman.

Table of Contents

Chapter 1
Birth and Medicine
In The Amish Family

To be born into an Old Order Amish family is to be born into a life filled with love, laughter, extremely hard work and very strict adherence to the Scriptures. The birth of a child is a joyous occasion in the lives of Amish couples and looked upon as a blessing from God. Child rearing and family life are the centerpieces of Amish home life and a large family is desirable. The use of birth control is strictly prohibited as it is considered to be interfering with the will of God and the average Amish couple will be the parents of seven or eight children.

The prenatal months are spent in preparing the layette in anticipation of the little one's arrival. The tiny dresses, jackets, bonnets, blankets and diapers are all hand-sewn during the pregnancy by the expectant mother and family members. There are no baby showers and parties to herald the arrival of a new baby. All of the baby's necessities are provided by family and friends. The pregnancy is not mentioned, nor is undue attention drawn to the expectant mother's condition. This is a very private matter and is not to be discussed. There is no need for special maternity clothing because the traditional Amish woman's dress is full-skirted and the waistband can be easily adjusted to accommodate the special cargo growing beneath. The baby will be given just a first name and a middle initial. The initial is the first letter of the father's name, so that all the children in one family have the same middle initial. For example, all the children of Eli and Lydia Troyer would have the middle initial E. The names might be Reuben E. Troyer, Mary E. Troyer, Daniel E. Troyer, Mose E. Troyer, Lizzie E. Troyer, Emma E. Troyer, Jacob E. Troyer, Levi E. Troyer, etc. This method of naming children helps to differentiate between families in this society where there are a limited number of surnames.

Usually, no formal prenatal care is sought early in routine pregnancies because the Amish do not consider being with child as an illness. Any information needed by the new mother is received from older women in the family who have had the experience of giving birth and are considered to be the experts. The expectant mother simply goes about her daily life as usual, taking care of the household chores and any other children in the family. During the final trimester of the pregnancy, some Amish women do seek prenatal care. In cases where difficulties arise, the Old Order Amish do not hesitate to see a doctor. When the time comes for the baby to make an appearance, many Amish women prefer to use the services of a midwife.

The midwife is a very important part of the Old Order Amish community because she makes it possible for the Amish women to have assisted births while remaining at home or in the local birthing center. The cost of a typical hospital stay is prohibitive to many of the Amish families, especially considering the size of the average Amish family. The midwife and local birthing facilities fill a void within the community. However, the governments of several states have, in recent years, attempted to put restrictions on the midwives and their centers, which have caused great concern among the Amish population. A well-known case in the area of western Pennsylvania and eastern Ohio involves Grace Lucille Sykes.

Lucy, as she prefers to be called, is an "English" woman who has served her community as a midwife since the mid-1970's. Before marrying and relocating to western Pennsylvania, she had grown up and attended public school and college in Washington state. After she and her husband arrived in Mercer County, Pennsylvania and established a home, they became well-acquainted with the local Amish women. As a result of these friendships the need for a midwife became obvious to Lucy. Although trained as a school teacher, she never had been in the classroom and the idea of aiding her friends as a midwife appealed to her. She traveled to Fredricksburg, Virginia for training and then came home to work with a practicing midwife in nearby New Wilmington, Pennsylvania for a two-year apprenticeship. During this apprenticeship she delivered the first of more than 1,000 babies. So thrilled to have their own midwife were the Amish in her area, that they got together and bought a small house which they had moved to a spot beside her residence. She is in constant demand and during one recent week, had six pending deliveries.

But, a local child welfare agency in her county began to investigate her birthing clinic and decided that she was practicing medicine without a license. They formally charged her with child abuse and the other charge and the Pennsylvania State Police went to her home to arrest her. What a furor there was among the Amish families for miles around! They were confident in Lucy's abilities and were especially pleased that her fee of $500.00 was just about one fourth of the cost of a hospital stay of just several hours for childbirth. And besides, she had never lost a baby, was competent and well-trained and always called in a medical doctor if there was a difficult birth.

Rallying behind her and her Amish friends was the Pennsylvania Midwives Association. Local support, even among the "English" population was strongly behind this woman who had given so much to the community. Fund-raising efforts ranged from tureen dinners to benefit auctions to square dances. Letter-writing campaigns were launched and the newspapers from miles away picked up the story from the wire services. Personal letters of support were received from Amish and Mennonite folks from all over the country.

When the case finally made its way to the courts, there was an over-flow crowd of spectators in the small-town courthouse in Mercer, Pennsylvania. Amish men and women came from miles around and many "English" supporters were there, as well. There was testimony from other midwives and the verdict was in Lucy's favor. On the walls of her Cradle Time Birthing Clinic are the names of each little bundle of joy she has delivered...more than 1,000 in all!

The Amish have many superstitions which have been passed down through the generations. Some of them have their origins in Europe and are shared by other cultures, as well. Because pregnancy and birth bring with them a great amount of risk and sacrifice, to both parents, there are myriad beliefs and superstitions concerning the birth of children. Some of them are:

"Put an old diaper on a newborn child, or it might become a thief.

The first dress put on a child should be new; an old one will cause it to be a 'slop'.

Place a horseshoe with nails in it in the child's cradle; it is conducive to good health.

To guard against a child being left-handed, it must be nursed the first time at the right breast.

The doctor or midwife, or whoever, should always use care to place the child's right arm in the sleeve first, to keep it from becoming left-handed.

Burn the first diaper for luck.

A person born in January will be able to see ghosts.

A child on its first day should be carried to the garret and allowed to look out the garret window if it is to become a respected citizen.

Payment of the doctor's fee in full will prevent the child from growing."[1]

Good health and well-being are of primary

---

[1]Monroe Aurand, Jr., <u>Popular Home Remedies and Superstitions of the Pennsylvania Germans</u>, (Harrisburg, Pennsylvania: The Aurand Press, 1941), 7.

importance to the Old Order Amish. They are concerned with the overall vitality of their family members and regularly seek professional help when they are not well. They seem to prefer the old-fashioned remedies and often treat their maladies with folk medicine and unconventional methods. This practice has resulted from centuries of using folk healing methods "proven" to be successful by word of mouth testimonials. Many of these remedies are remnants of those used by their ancestors in combination with those learned from their "English" (any person who is not Amish is called English, regardless of their family tree) neighbors. They are more apt to seek cures than to employ preventive measures and they use any number of poultices, extracts, vitamins, tonics, herb teas and homemade concoctions to gain relief. They tend to rely on these treatments rather than go to the doctor's office, unless the condition worsens.

One source of some of the long-used and, perhaps, now long-forgotten, folk remedies used by the Amish in centuries past, lists for us the following ailments and cures:

AGUE...If you would be "shut" of the ague, drink of your own urine.

BEDWETTING...A child who is more or less an habitual bedwetter should "piddle" into a grave covered that day; time, after dusk; or fried mouse or mouse pie cures bedwetting, or if burned to ashes and the ashes secretly put into coffee, tea or other drink will cure.

COLD IN THE HEAD...This is an old cure. Pass your finger over your "hind-end" and smell it. For cold in the head and chest, we know of a case where fresh hog dung was steamed and the vapor inhaled by a very sick patient in the upper part of Dauphin County, (Pennsylvania) who had been "given up" by the doctor; the patient recovered, much to the surprise of all, and later it appears in medical circles that there was more than a little bit of merit in the cure.

FRECKLES...Remove freckles by washing them with the water of baptism. Or, with water collected from tombstones. If it rains on you while there is a rainbow, you will get freckles.

HEADACHE...If you would prevent a headache, or toothache, you must form the habit of putting on your right stocking, first; your right shoe, etc. During dog days, if rain falls on your head, look out for baldness or headache.

HERNIA...To reduce it use a sadiron. Another cure: get a gorged nail, drive it in wood, and keep it in a dry place.

HICCOUGHS...For this uncomfortable and annoying disturbance, sit down, with a glass of water by your side; let someone put a little water in each ear with the little finger of each hand, keeping the fingers there until you have drunk all the water. Another: Bend forward so that the hands touch the ground and say, "O hiccough, I wish that you were in my buttocks.

MUMPS...It is a common practice to persuade one afflicted with mumps to enter a pig sty, and rub the swollen neck a certain odd number of times on the front edge of the hog-trough, which was worn smooth by the necks of the feeding swine.

NOSEBLEED...In modern times, for nosebleed, one can chew newspaper. Another cure:

Try to recall who sat next to you the last time you were in church, if you can!

SCRATCH OR CUT...You can sterilize a wound by sucking it with your mouth; or, if not, if you can urinate on it this also sterilizes.

SORE THROAT...Wear one of your long stockings around your neck, with the foot under your chin. Or, drag your finger between your toes and inhale deeply.

WARTS...Rub warts with pebbles and throw them in a grave; or rub warts with the blood of a chicken which has nothing but black feathers; or a piece of potato, which must be buried under the eaves; or use soft green walnuts; or the hand of a corpse; or, beans; or, the head of a rooster that has just been killed; or the rind of bacon, which is then hung on a tree so the birds may eat it. Pow-wowers use saliva. Scratch a wart with a nail taken from a coffin, until it bleeds; it will then disappear."[2]

They are not averse to visit medical practitioners and specialists of all types. They use the services of physicians, chiropractors, homeopaths (who treat the disease by producing symptoms similar to that of the disease), pow-wow doctors (who use charms, amulets and chants to cure the ailment) and reflexologists (who manipulate the feet to cure ailments of the rest of the body). They prefer to be seen by the small town general practitioner and usually have a good rapport with those in the medical field. Occasionally a doctor in an Amish community makes house calls which is a great help to an Amish family who must travel to an English neighbor's house or to a roadside pay telephone to contact the doctor and then go to the doctor's office via horse and buggy if treatment is suggested. One such country doctor is Dr. Roy Miller of Holmes County, Ohio. Dr. Miller has two offices

---

[2] Ibid., 10.

and a pharmacy in the midst of the largest Amish and Mennonite population in the entire world. He lives just a few miles from a hospital but has the equipment to do many procedures in his office. Fifty percent of his patients are Amish.[3]

There are no known Amish physicians or chiropractors, basically because of their concern that higher education leads to worldliness and the opportunity to earn much more than subsistence level income. There are reflexologists among the Amish. However, the skills required to successfully treat clients are learned "on the job" and through seminars and workshops of short duration. The services of these practitioners is widely sought and they frequently have more appointments than they can meet. Payment is a donation rather than a fee. Because Amish do not generally believe in health insurance, the cost of medical treatment is often a deterrent. Their objection to such coverage is based on the belief that commercial companies are reliant on the law and would weaken the community's mutual aid tenets. They hold to the belief that it is their duty to take care of their own in times of distress and need. The church sees to it that no one goes without the care needed and extended families provide this care with the aid of the other church members.

Although there is no written rule prohibiting vaccination, there has been a reluctance among the Amish to have their children immunized against the childhood diseases. They tend to concentrate on symptoms they have experienced rather than the possibility of an unfamiliar disease they have never known to occur. Therefore, most Amish children have not been immunized against diphtheria, tetanus, polio, measles or mumps. Most states require proof that these vaccines have been administered before a child may start school, but there are exemptions for those who object to the immunizations for religious reasons. These exemption forms are used by those Amish parents who insist that the vaccine is not necessary.

However, the Amish community does respond when the

---

[3] Country Doctor Caters to Amish," The Youngstown Vindicator, 28 March 1993.

threat of an outbreak occurs. During 1979 a polio epidemic in the Netherlands prompted a wide-spread immunization program among the unvaccinated Amish children in Pennsylvania. The polio virus can go undetected for long periods of time and travel for thousands of miles during that time. For every case of polio that is diagnosed, there are 1,000 cases which develop no symptoms or get diagnosed. The people who are undiagnosed carry and transmit the virus without knowing they have it. As a result of that epidemic ten Americans, eight of them Amish in Pennsylvania, contracted the disease and were paralyzed. During the winter of 1992, there was another outbreak of polio in the Netherlands which World Health Organization and Centers for Disease Control officials feared would make its way into the United States. In Pennsylvania, the Department of Health sent letters to the more than 100 Amish and Mennonite bishops in rural communities asking them to permit large-scale polio immunizations of their members. (A similar program was initiated in Iowa by that state's Department of Public Health.) The Department wanted to set up free clinics in the areas with large Amish populations and felt they needed the powerful bishops as allies in the cause. As a follow-up to the letters, Health Department officials visited the bishops to reinforce the necessity of immunizing the unvaccinated population. The bishops were convinced of the danger to their people and permitted the Health Department to set up the clinics and spread the word to the population that immunization would be allowed. According to Health Department officials in western Pennsylvania, the response was not as significant as they had anticipated. This was primarily because many more of the Amish had been vaccinated than was previously believed. This seems to indicate that education about the need for immunization is having the desired effect. There was also a small group of Old Order Amish who flatly refused to be immunized. For whatever reason, there was not one diagnosed case of polio in that area. Although the threat of polio seems to be behind the Amish community, Pennsylvania Health Department officials are currently concerned about measles and whooping cough. At this time there are no plans to attempt large-scale immunizations as was done in 1979 and in 1992.

A study of health-care practices of the Lancaster County, Pennsylvania Amish was conducted during 1978 by Johns Hopkins Hospital. The findings, as reported by noted Amish sociologist, Dr. John Hostetler, follow:

> The survey was conducted among 100 married women between the ages of twenty and forty-five who had given birth during the previous year. The sources of their health care were reported as follows: 76% of the respondents had visited a medically trained doctor, while 20% had visited "alternative" practitioners. The latter category included chiropractors, homeopaths, pow-wow doctors and reflexologists. The "alternative" practitioners, however, had been visited more frequently than the medically trained doctors. Only 26% of the children had been immunized against diphtheria, whooping and tetanus; 23% had been immunized against polio; and 16% had been give immunization against measles and mumps. The survey was completed before the 1979 and 1992 outbreaks of polio.
>
> Of the 472 pregnancies reported in the survey, there had been 55 miscarriages and 3 stillbirths, or a fetal loss rate of 12%. Ninety percent of the first births had occurred in a hospital, while 59% of the "last births" had been home deliveries. The average cost of a home delivery was $272, while hospital deliveries averaged $750. Although many children were born at home, 22% of the women did not seek prenatal care until the sixth month of pregnancy."[4]

---

[4]John Hostetler, <u>Amish Society</u> (Baltimore: Johns Hopkins University Press, 1980), 317.

The Amish have provided genetic researchers with some very challenging and intriguing projects over the decades. One such study deals with a strange trait shared by the Amish in Lancaster County, Pennsylvania and the aborigines in western Australia. The abnormality, being born with an extra finger or toe (polydactylism), is rare in most all parts of the world. In November, 1992, the *Medical Journal of Australia* published a report by Dr. Jack Goldblatt concluding that the high incidence of the six-finger or six-toe condition, a symptom of Ellis-van Creveld (EVC) syndrome, among the Amish and the aborigines stems from a common European ancestor. Goldblatt surmised that the gene reached North America and western Australia from a Dutch ancestor aboard the Dutch sailing ship, *Zuytdorp*, which was wrecked off the west coast of Australia in 1712. The survivors had gone ashore and joined aboriginal tribes.[5]

Another genetic disorder within the Old Order Mennonite (a sect closely related to and sharing their origins with the Old Order Amish) population of Pennsylvania is referred to as Maple Sugar Urine Disease (MSUD). This disease occurs when certain amino acids are not properly metabolized and build up in the body, resulting in urine that smells sugary and is accompanied by a number of neurological problems. A rare condition in the general population, one in every 176 Old Order Mennonite baby is afflicted with MSUD. The disease is fatal in a large percentage of cases, even when dietary therapy is used. The children who survive have lower than average IQ's and are underdeveloped. Scientists are currently working on a cure for MSUD using sophisticated gene-therapy to cause the amino acids to be properly metabolized in the body.[6]

Although the non-competitive, peace-loving and close to the soil existence of the Amish does tend to make for lower stress levels than the general population, they are not without mental illness. Anxiety and depression are found among the Amish and

[5]"Aborigines, Amish Share Strange Extra-toe Trait" The Youngstown Vindicator, 26 November 1992.
[6]"The Curse of the Mennonites", Discover, 1 October 1993.

a high degree of frustration can build up when there is no acceptable way to relieve the tension through aggressive means. Both men and women will seek treatment and often take prescribed tranquilizers to relieve the condition. Generally, the Amish persons suffering with mental illness are cared for in the home, using the basic therapy of outpourings of love and bolstering of self-esteem. However, if institutionalization becomes necessary, there are facilities run basically by and for the Amish and Mennonites. In Maryland there is Brook Lane Hospital, established in 1948; in Pennsylvania, Philhaven Hospital, founded in 1952 and in Elkhart, Indiana, there is Oaklawn Psychiatric Center. Although these hospitals serve persons of all faiths, they are self-sustaining and are operated by Mennonites.[7]

Just as in any cross-section of society there are occasionally among the Amish tragic consequences of mental illness. Such is the case of Edward Gingerich, of Crawford County, Pennsylvania, an Old Order Amishman with a wife and three small children. On March 18, 1993, Gingerich, then 27, savagely murdered his wife, Katie, who was 29, by smashing her skull and slashing and disemboweling her body. The act was made all the more horrendous by the fact that two of the Gingerich's three children, a three-year-old daughter and a five-year-old son witnessed their father's unspeakable act. This was the first documented case of an Amishman committing a murder in more than a century. At the trial, the defense argued that Mr. Gingerich was suffering from mental disorders. He admitted to the slaying, admitted that he knew that two of his children were present when the brutal killing was taking place and admitted that he knew his wife was dead when he had finished. However, for a year before the slaying, Gingerich complained of "disorientation" and severe headaches. He had been taken to a mental hospital in Jamestown, New York, on more than one occasion. He was treated for schizophrenia and given medication which he stopped taking after he returned home and began to "feel better". According to

<hr>

[7]Hostetler, 322.

his father,[8] Gingerich felt that God had deserted him and he had become possessed by the devil when his headaches became increasingly more severe. On the day of the crime he had sought treatment from a chiropractor. Dr. Merritt Terrell testified that he had given Gingerich a scalp massage and told him to drink blackstrap molasses just hours before the slaying. Later, the couple argued and their oldest child, a 6-year-old son, was sent by his mother to a brother-in-law's house nearby. According to testimony at the trial, the boy told his uncle, "Come quick, Dad's sick!" Edward's brother, Daniel, Jr., arrived at the scene of the crime to find a blood-covered Edward sitting on his wife's eviscerated body. A knife was lying on the floor near the body. He ran to an "English" neighbor's house to phone the authorities. When rescue personnel and police arrived, Edward Gingerich was walking down the dirt lane leading from his farmhouse, carrying his daughter and holding his younger son by the hand. When the arresting officer approached him, Edward Gingerich said, "I am the bad guy you are looking for."[9]

The court appointed attorney for Gingerich entered a plea of guilty by reason of insanity and eventually was able to get the charges reduced from murder to guilty of involuntary manslaughter but mentally ill. The judge held Gingerich accountable and at fault for not seeking further treatment for his mental illness, and sentenced him to the maximum allowable by law. He is currently serving 2 1/2 to 5 years in the State Penitentiary in Pittsburgh. His father reportedly stated, "All we can do is pray for him. It's just so unusual, we don't know what else to do."[10] As the Amish community prayed for Edward Gingerich and his uncle, the bishop, was quoted in an Associated Press story as saying, "One thing for sure, this wasn't God's work. But it's not for us to judge him. God will judge him."

---

[8]Claudia Coates, "Beliefs Complicate Case," The Herald, 21 March 1994.
[9]Amish Man Sought Help, Found None", The Herald, 24 March 1994.
[10]Suspect in Amish Slaying Showed Behavioral Problems", The Greenville Record Argus, 29 March 1993.

Chapter 2
Amish Childhood

In Old Order Amish culture, having babies and raising them to be God's children is a fundamental goal. The arrival of a child is considered to be a blessing from God and that child is loved and nurtured by all of the family and community members. The baby is received into the family as an innocent and blameless little one who is not yet responsible for any wrongdoing or sinfulness. From the very beginning of the child's life he/she is respected and revered as a gift from God and enjoyed by all. The infant spends most of its first year of life being held and rocked by family members and friends. The child is almost never put down and allowed to spend time alone while the rest of the household goes about its business. A crying baby is thought to be in need of attention and is either hungry or is experiencing some other form of discomfort. There is usually no feeding schedule because babies are fed when they are hungry. They are never disciplined because they are crying. The baby who becomes spoiled is that way by some sort of inappropriate handling by an adult and is not to blame. There is no infant baptism in the Amish religion, as they believe that the decision to accept the Lord and live the very, very uncompromising life of an Amish person is one that must not be taken lightly, nor can the decision be made for another. Thus, the children are raised in the way of the church and the hope is that each of them will be so strong in their faith, that they will make the decision to join the church and take their baptismal vows when they are in their late teens or early twenties.

Those outside the Amish community are taken by the "quaintness" of the children's clothing, which is identical to that of their parents. One of the most important things about Amish dress is that the attire is one of the most obvious symbols setting them apart from the rest of the world. They have retained much the same style of clothing that they wore in the Palatine region of Switzerland during the sixteenth century. The plain, but functional garb continues to serve their needs and sets them apart from the worldliness that threatens their existence. The similarity of dress also discourages pride and encourages modesty and signifies that the wearer is an integral part of the culture and religious group called the Old Order Amish. The changes that have occurred down through the centuries are more to do with practicality than keeping up with the styles of the rest of the world. As the textile industry introduced labor-saving fabrics that required much less care, the church officials recognized the need to permit their people to use those fabrics. There can be no modification, though, by the members of a community. The church officials set the rules and the people must adhere.

All children are dressed alike until they reach the age of sixteen months to two years. They are attired in miniature dresses just like the ones worn by their older sisters. They consist of a basic long-sleeved, high-necked bodice with a gathered, ankle-length skirt. An A-line, sleeveless apron with one button at the back of the neck is put on over the dress. The front of the dress is held together by straight pins or hooks and eyes, but never with buttons or safety pins. There are several theories concerning the absence of buttons on most Amish clothing. One speculation is that buttons have their origin in the military and the Amish are strictly non-violent pacifists. Another is that the buttons would be decorative and therefore worldly. A widely held story is that the buttons would give the devil a place to hang on and that, of course would be forbidden. There is no conclusive research to support any one of these reasons for prohibiting the use of buttons, but all of them have some credibility. One thing is an absolute. There are never buttons on the clothing of the Old Order Amish women and the ones that appear on the men's and children's clothing are very strictly regulated. The straight pin vs. hook and eye decision is made by the bishop of the church district and is not subject to change. The older girls and women have a cape or *Halsduch* over the bodice of their dresses and an apron, instead of the one-piece apron of the girls under eight years old. This cape is made of a triangular piece of fabric 30 inches long. The point is fastened at the back of the waist with straight pins. The two long pieces go up over the shoulders and cross in the front. These ends are pinned at the waist, also. This cape is a practical covering for the breasts and is present to encourage modesty. It also makes it much easier for the nursing mother to feed her baby discreetly, in most any setting. The apron is several inches shorter than the dress and is fastened to a belt of one to four inches wide. The width signifies the permissiveness of the church community, with the narrow waistbands the mark of the more conservative members. The apron belt is fastened at the front and at the back of the waist with straight pins. Ties and pockets are not permitted on the apron, as they would be considered too showy, or worldly. There are patch pockets on the skirt of the women's dresses, but they are hidden from view by the apron. Amish girls and women wear dresses of brightly colored fabrics in shades of powder blue, royal blue or navy blue, green, turquoise, purple, plum, gray and more subdued browns. Reds, pinks, oranges and yellows are prohibited, as are patterned fabrics. The dress and the cape and apron are all the same solid color for everyday, and for church the cape and apron are white organdy. A bride always wears a white dress, apron and cape for her wedding day, the same ones she will probably wear to be laid out in when she passes on. The women wear black dresses for communion services, funerals and during mourning periods. For winter, the older girls and women wear long wool shawls which are triangles of fabric which go around the shoulders and are fastened at the front with a hatpin or a safety pin. Younger girls wear homemade wool coats to school and for play.

Jewelry, of any type, is forbidden for Amish women. A wedding ring is not needed, according to their teachings, because they make a vow with God at their wedding and do not need outward symbols of the bond.

A headcovering for the girls is a requirement from the age of six weeks when they attend their first worship service. This *Kapp* is white organdy has a number of variations in pleating, length of ties, width of bands in the front and back among church communities. The only exception to this is that girls from twelve years of age until when they get married wear a black *Kapp* for Sunday church services and a white one at home. The girls and women wear a black bonnet over their organdy headcovering when they go anywhere in public, and especially in cold weather. The bonnet is similar to the old-fashioned sunbonnets worn by the farm women of the nineteenth century. It is made of black fabric and the wide brim nearly hides the profile of the wearer. The girls and women never have their hair cut and it is always worn parted in the middle, combed straight back from the face, rolled tightly along the head and fashioned into a bun at the base of the neck. Sometimes the young girls' hair is braided and tucked under the headcovering, but never are the braids allowed to hang freely. Their hair is never worn loose or curled. Even when doing manual labor, the Amish females' hair will be covered, but the covering may be a scarf or bandanna when hard and dirty work is involved.

When the boys are about one and one half years old, they are dressed in their first pair of pants, which have buttonholes at the waist to attach to the buttons on the shirt. The little boys are dressed this way until they are about four. Then they are dressed in the style of the adult men. They wear the "broadfall" or "barndoor" denim trousers with two large overlapping panels in the front which button to the waist instead of having a fly. The reason for this style is to encourage modesty. The number and size of buttons are determined by the bishop. These trousers have no pockets in back, but there are pockets on either side. Belts are never worn, and suspenders, if anything, are used to hold up the trousers. The suspenders are of cloth or leather and may be of a variety of styles and widths, also at the discretion of the bishop and other church officials. They are worn for modesty, so that the pants do not have to fit tightly. The use of rubber is permitted only for boots and galoshes. The shirts of the men are made from the same fabrics as the girls' and women's dresses, have a front pocket, with buttons, are collarless and have long sleeves. They wear a black vest and frock coat or *Mutze*, with split tails, over a white shirt to the preaching service and a shorter, less tailored coat, for daily wear. The jackets have no lapels and have stand-up collars. There are no outside pockets on these jackets. The coats and vests are fastened by hooks and eyes, never buttons. Men are not permitted to wear neckties, nor are they ever to wear striped or patterned shirts. A pocket watch is permitted, but a wristwatch and all other jewelry are forbidden. The men and boys wear a broad-brimmed black felt hat in the winter and a similarly styled straw one during the warmer weather. The hats are kept, in some homes, in a hat press. The press is made from plywood and consists of a flat board, the width of the brim, to which is attached, by hinges, a similar-sized piece of wood with the center cut out to accommodate the crown of the hat. The hat is placed on the bottom piece of wood, the lid is closed and the brim is flattened and straightened. For their "Sunday hats," a similar press is used, but with the addition of a form to keep the crown portion of the hat clean and properly shaped, as well. The crown shape and brim width of the Amishmen's straw and felt hats are indications of which church district they belong to, because these details are the bishop's decision and all must conform to the standard. The boys and men have "bowl" hairstyles, cut to the mid-to-bottom of the ear, with "bangs" straight across and halfway down the forehead. The young men are clean-shaven until they either become baptized and join the church, or get married. This may vary slightly from community to community and is the decision of the church leaders. After that time, the men grow beards, which are never trimmed, but they always have a clean-shaven upper lip. Moustaches are prohibited. In virtually all Amish communities an unmarried man over the age of forty must also grow a beard.

The children also go barefoot in the summer and both boys and girls wear black hightop shoes when the weather is too cold for barefeet. The girls wear opaque black stockings with their shoes. Older girls and women will often be seen in low-cut black "tennis" shoes or black leather low-heeled oxfords.

The clothing styles are clearly defined within the *Ordnung*, or rules of the church. This document contains regulations for nearly every facet of Amish life and varies slightly from one district to another, depending upon how liberal the district is. What follows is the part of an *Ordnung* published by a church in Pike County, Ohio, which delineates the physical appearance of the Old Order Amish:

> No ornamental, bright, showy, form-fitting, immodest or silk-like clothing of any kind. Colors such as bright red, orange, yellow and pink are not allowed. Amish form of clothing to be followed as a general rule. Costly Sunday clothing to be discouraged. Dresses not shorter than half-way between knees and floor, not eight inches from the floor. Longer advisable. Clothing in every way modest, serviceable and as simple as scripturally possible. Only outside pockets are allowed on work eberhem or vomas and pockets on large overcoats. Dress shoes, if any, plain and black only. No high heels and pomp (sic) slippers, dress socks, if any, to be black, except white for foot hygiene for both sexes. A plain, unshowy suspender without buckles.

Hat to be black with no less than 3-inch rim and not extremely high in crown. No stylish impression in any hat, No pressed trousers. No sweater.

Prayer covering to be simple, made to fit the head. Should cover all the hair as nearly as possible and is to be worn whenever possible. No silk ribbons. Young children to dress accordingly to the Word as well as parents. No pink or fancy baby blankets or caps.

A full beard should be worn among men and boys after baptism, if possible. No shingled hair. Length at least half-way below tops of ears.[1]

The child is usually part of a large immediate family and an even larger extended family and soon becomes trained and nurtured in the way of *Gelassenheit,* or the giving up of oneself to be suited to do God's will. The elements of *Gelassenheit* have been described by Donald B. Kraybill as follows:

Personality: Reserved, modest, calm, quiet
Values: Submission, obedience, humility, simplicity
Symbols: Dress, horse, carriage, lantern
Structure: Small, informal, local, decentralized
Ritual: Baptism, confession, ordination, footwashing[2]

The large number of people in the family make it necessary for the children to wait their turn, or to acquiesce to the others, a basic lesson which must be learned very early. The discipline is strict and is imposed from the age of about two, when it is thought that the child is capable of understanding the restrictions. In the words of one Amish leader, "By the time the child reaches the age of three the mold has started to form and it is the parents' duty to form it in the way that the child should go. When the child is old enough to stiffen its back and throw back its head

[1] Amish Church of Pike County, Ohio, "*Ordnung* of a Christian Church", n.d.
[2] Donald B. Kraybill, The Riddle of Amish Culture (Baltimore: The Johns Hopkins University Press, 1989), 26.

in temper, it is old enough to gently start breaking that temper."[3] The parents' authority is never questioned and is absolute. Respect for their elders is learned by Amish children at an early age and is constantly reinforced. Along with the uncompromising discipline is an unconditional love from the parents and other family members. Theirs is not a totally idyllic lifestyle and they do experience some of the ills of society as a whole, but to a much lesser extent. Sibling rivalry exists, of course, but is dealt with more quietly than it usually is in other segments of society. The loud and heated verbal exchanges so common among children are rarely heard because the Amish child learns passive resistance from an early age. Profanity is absolutely forbidden and the punishment is swift and severe if a child or young person is heard taking the Lord's name in vain. Children learn at an early age that they are expected to behave in a certain way and there is no room for discussion. They also learn that the rewards for living up to their elders' expectations are peace of mind and total acceptance within a loving family circle. Although the children in a Amish family are expected to obey and submit to their elders, there are times when discipline is necessary. The Amish, like the "English," are given advice on child-rearing by a number of experts. One such Amish writer has offered some basics of discipline which seem to have much merit. The anonymous writer penned these words in 1882:

> Why are children disobedient? The question, we know, is one that many troubled parents have wondered about. Part of the answer lies in the Adamic nature of the child, but part of it, also, is the fault of the parents, who have failed to train the child as they should. This failure in training may stem from ignorance, as well as from an unconcerned attitude. The following are some reasons why some children are disobedient:
>
> 1. Instructions are not always stated in the way

---

[3]Guidelines in Regards to the Old Order Amish and Parochial Schools (Gordonville, Pennsylvania: Gordonville Print Shop, 1981), 50.

they should be. The child does not feel the parents mean what they say, or that the command is to be obeyed to the word.

2. Promises are frequently made to the children, but they are not kept. This encourages disobedience.

3. A threat of punishment is made, but is not carried out. The child loses respect for the parents.

4. The parent forbids something, yet later allows the child to have it, because the child has cried. Many a child is master of his parents through his crying.

5. Immediate obedience is not insisted upon as it should be. Putting things off until later has brought great trouble, and will bring great trouble in this instance.

6. The parents need to explain to the child that disobedience to father or mother is also disobedience to God, and that it is a sin before God to disobey.

7. Too much is expected from the child. The parent gives the command, but fails to explain how it should be carried out. The child loses heart.

8. The child sees that disobedience makes his parents angry, whereas it should make him sorrowful. Let the child know that his misdeeds sadden your heart, but never anger you.

9. Prayer is too often neglected. The best rules fail if God does not give his blessing. And his spirit is the only thing that can bring true obedience. A good rule for training children, as for anything else, is--"Pray and Labor."[4]

---

[4]Anonymous, "*Herold der Wahrheit*" (January 15, 1882), in John A. Hostetler, Editor, <u>Amish Roots; A Treasury of History, Wisdom and Lore</u>, (Baltimore: The Johns Hopkins University Press, 1989), 111-112.

The personalities of the children are much different from those of children in non-Amish societies. John Hostetler conducted a study of personality traits among Amish children and found that they exhibit the characteristics of *Gelassenheit*. The Amish child is "...quiet, friendly, responsible and conscientious. (He) works devotedly to meet his obligations and serve his friends and school...(he is) patient with detail and routine. (He is) loyal, considerate, concerned with how other people feel even when they are in the wrong."[5]

There are clearly defined ages and stages of the Amish person's life, beginning with the "baby stage". That phase lasts from birth until the child begins to walk. The phrase "little children" is used to describe the ones who are walking until the time they enter school. "Scholars" are the ones in school, usually age 6 through 15, and "young people" are adolescents who are through with school until they are married.[6] From a very early age, the offspring of an Amish couple are expected to do their share of the work in the home and on the farm or in the father's workplace. The girls are taught the skills of homemaking by their mother, grandmother and older sisters. These skills involve cooking; baking; gardening; canning; sewing, including making all of the shirts, pants, coats, dresses, aprons, capes, *Kapps* and underwear worn by the family and quilting, as well; washing and ironing (using a sadiron which has been heated on the cookstove); cleaning and maintaining the kerosene lamps that are used for light in the home and caring for the younger children. The boys are sent to work with their fathers and grandfathers as soon as they are old enough. The Amish were first an agrarian society and many of them are still farmers today. The farm work is done without the aid of mechanized tractors and equipment to help with the planting and harvesting. All of the field work is done by horse-drawn machinery. Even small children have a responsibility to work the land and girls, as well

[5]John Hostetler, "Educational Achievement and Lifestyles in a Traditional Society, the Old Order Amish", Temple University, Philadelphia, Pennsylvania, 1969.
[6]John Hostetler, Amish Society, 1980, 173.

as boys, are taught at an early age how to cultivate the corn or plow a straight furrow. The small children, from the age of four to six, are trained to be of help to the family and have some small responsibilities. The little boys are taught to feed the chickens and gather the eggs, feed the baby animals and relate to the horses. The little girls learn to help their mother with setting the table, washing and drying dishes and other household tasks. Although many of the skills learned by the children as they are growing up are gender-oriented, some things are, of necessity, done by both sexes. Girls are often in the barn helping with the chores, or in the fields, planting and harvesting right along with the boys. The girls are taught to harness the horses and drive the buggy or farm machinery. The boys may also be found in the house or garden, doing dishes, setting the table or weeding the large family garden. All of the school-age children must get their morning chores finished up before they have their breakfast and set out on the walk to school.

Within the community, of necessity, are craftsmen and business people who provide goods and services to their peers. These include the harness makers; the cabinetmakers; the tinners; buggy manufacturers; the drygoods dealers, who provide the denim, chambray, organdy and other fabrics needed to make the clothing and quilts of the Amish, as well as bulk food items and staples used in the homes; machinery builders and repairers to list just the basic ones.

When the chores are done and there is time for leisure, the Amish family often visits family members or friends in the community. While the adults discuss the goings on of the community and the health of their family and friends, the children may be off to the backyard to play a rough and tumble game of softball, hide and seek, tag or blindman's bluff. Some may end up in the barn to play basketball, ping pong or corner ball, a favorite game. Many of the games they play are the same games our ancestors played when they were growing up during the last century. Some toys, such as wagons, riding toys and balls and bats are "store bought", but many of the things Amish children play with are things found around the house or barn. A favorite pastime for young boys is to "harness" one another with leftover baling twine and play "horse", imitating their mode of transportation.

Both the boys and girls have the opportunity to build things as they are growing up. The girls like to make things for their playhouses and the boys make birdfeeders, birdhouses and toys. The boys also enjoy the outdoor pastimes of hunting, trapping and fishing. Although they dislike direct involvement with the English and their laws, they do comply with the licensing regulations and wear the blaze orange clothing required for deer hunters.

When the days grow shorter and the temperatures fall, the fun moves inside. The lack of televisions, radios and CD players does not mean the winter evenings are long and boring. Jigsaw puzzles and board games like parcheesi and checkers are brought out to challenge the young people and reading material is always available in the Amish home. The books are usually the "old-fashioned" titles written when times were simpler and the Amish lifestyle was the norm. The stories are tales that extol the Christian virtues and are never fairy tales, tales of magic or stories in which animals have human characteristics. They might also gather around the kitchen table for a lesson in reading the scriptures in German. The German dialect that is spoken in the Amish home is different from the "high German" used in the Bible. The scholars may have homework to do and some of the adolescent girls might help their mother catch up on some mending or quilting. But bedtime comes early when the roosters crow at 4:30 or 5 a.m. signaling the start of another day, and everyone is usually more than ready to turn in for the night.

For the Amish young people, there are only two real decisions to be made about their future lives...whether to become baptized, and whom to marry. They have been raised to be God's children and their childhoods have provided long and intense preparation for their lives as Amish adults. They have learned the fundamental doctrines of the Old Order Amish Church and they know what is expected of them. But, there is still time to sow some wild oats and live a little more worldly sort of life between the end of their formal education and the day they become church members. This coming of age period is referred to as *Rum springa*, or running around. The boys typically reach this stage at about fifteen or sixteen and the girls a year or two earlier, at thirteen or fourteen. This period of an Amish teenager's life is one of introspection and questioning. They all know that their parents and friends and relatives in the church community expect each one of them to make the "right" choice and become baptized. But the decision is a difficult one for many Amish youth. The more they are exposed to the trappings of the worldly "English" lifestyle, the more burdensome it may become. It is during this period that the parents rely on the young person's upbringing and the strong ties of the church, the home and the family to steer him/her to the correct choice. The young men, especially, are given a great deal of freedom. They are often presented with their own horse and buggy when they reach sixteen, just as many "English" youth are given a car to drive when they are sixteen and get a driver's license. They run around in groups called "gangs" or "crowds" and sometimes the behavior becomes quite boisterous. The crowds develop an attitude or personality, which ranges from very conservative and tame to much more liberal and rowdy. The membership is informal and can number as many as 300, although the more typical number is 100.[7] The young people plan many activities as groups and the crowd becomes the focus of their social life. Many Amish boys also use the opportunity *Rum springa* gives them to buy a car and hide it somewhere out of sight of their parents and the church officials. They may also purchase "English"-style clothing and change into the worldly duds away from the farm and go out on the town. Many of them cut their hair

[7]Kraybill, 138

shorter than is permitted in what seems like a flaunting gesture to their elders. Drinking is also a problem among some of the Amish young people, just as it is among young people in every other cross-section of society. Donald Kraybill has written of a situation in which township officials wrote to church leaders to enlist their help in controlling the problem. The letter to the bishop asked him,"...to do all in your power to correct the drinking and drunkenness that presently prevails among Amish youth...according to records, the last fatal accidents that occurred in Leacock Township were either the direct results of, or involved drinking Amish youth." The bishops of the area, in response to the plea, met and agreed upon five points of an *Ordnung* which, in rare fashion, was published.[8] Some of the Amish youth present great challenges to their parents when the are in this stage and it can cause some dissention among family members. But church officials tolerate these actions and look the other way while the youth of the church get a taste of the flashy, exciting world outside their own. The hope is, and it would seem they are right about this, that all those years of training and learning the ways of the Old Order Amish lifestyle will prevail and the young people will see that the Amish way is the only way to live. The church leaders are embarrassed by the young people's antics which seem like a complete contradiction in their lives, but there is little they can do to curb the behavior because the unbaptized are not subject to the rules of the church. Many "English" wonder why such behavior is tolerated when the lifestyle has been so very strict and severe before that phase of the child's life. The bishop and other leaders feel very strongly that their young people must have a chance to spread their wings before they take the vows and become baptized, for the consequences of breaking the sacred vows are much more dire than the risk that a small percentage (less than 20 %) of them will leave the church community totally.

Child rearing is the most important job of an Amish couple,

---

[8]Kraybill, 276.

and advice is often sought from other parents when problems do arise. A group of "Amish parents who have a concern for the on-coming generation" have compiled a list of rules for parents, which appeared in a recent issue of "Family Life."

Things To Do BEFORE Your Children Grow Up

Train up a child in the way he should go, and when he is old, he will not depart from it (*Proverbs 22:6*).

"These words, which I command thee shall be in thine heart and thou shall teach them diligently unto the children, and shalt talk of them when thou sittest in thine house and when thou walkest by the way and when thou liest down, and when thou risest up"
(*Deut. 22:5-6*).

We must be by example what we want our children to be. Children are great imitators. Your example is of utmost importance.

Be a parent, not just a playmate, but do play and pray together. If you love your children, then let *idleness* be counted as a sin in your family.

Be sure you have confidence in your children and they in you.

Let them know you are for them and not against them.

Be as good as your word if you want them to be as good as their word.

Work along with your children in their work and take an interest in what they do, or they may lose interest in what they do.

Pray for your children. The genuineness of your prayers will teach them the reality of God.

Devotions should not merely be an instruction period, but rather adoration, praise, love and appreciation of God.

Songs of praise magnify the wonders of God.

When conditions are as they should be in the home, it is a foretaste of Heaven.

As fathers and mothers, grandfathers and grandmothers, we have the biggest job in the world to teach our children to love the Lord.

Disobedience and disrespect for the parents are often the first steps downward that children take.

No man who dishonors father or mother ever prospers in the long run.

Isaac was so holy before his children, that when Jacob remembered God, he remembered him in the "fear of his father Isaac" (Gen. 31:53).

When parents err in their judgment and later recognize and confess it, they gain the respect of the child.

Unity between the parents is a must. When one parent says something, the other should back him up.

Study the Bible; acquaint your children with the simple truths of the Word.

There must be much gentleness and patience along with instructions, "lest they become discouraged" (Col. 3:21).

It always pays to speak kindly, especially to husband, wife or children.

If parents want the gratitude of their children, let them talk to them as though they were human beings. "Like begets like."

Love produces love and hatred produces hatred. It is usually the scolding parents who are disrespected by their children. Reproofs should always be given in gentle tones.

These do not belong in a Christian home: slang, vulgarity, frivolity, uncourteous treatment of youngsters, disrespect for elders, talking back to parents.

Never compare your child with other children. If you compare them favorably, they may become proud, if unfavorably, discouraged.

As soon as children show anger, they are old enough to be punished. A child will not desire to touch a hot stove more than once or twice. Our discipline should follow the same pattern.

A child is not trained properly until he obeys when told the first time, without question, and without the need for the parent to raise his voice.

Use discipline to correct your child, be fair but be firm.

Mother shall help faithfully, but Father must shoulder the blame if the training of the children is not accomplished.

If the woman has the lead in the conversation too much in the home, it is evidence that she is out of God's order: Christ, man, then woman.

In the sight of God it is much better for the woman to be of a meek and quiet spirit (I Peter 3:3-4).

Demanding obedience to satisfy every selfish whim or acting like a slave driver without due respect for the children, cannot be tolerated in the Christian home. Children will quickly discern whether or not we mean what we say.

When children are old enough to understand, they should be taught the basic facts about sex and reproduction of life before they learn it from a perverted source in an unscriptural manner.

Young people may develop sinful habits because they are not aware of the meaning of the impulses within them. A knowledge of the facts of life can help them from getting into habits which may trouble them for life.

Buying everything he wants results in a spoiled child. The parents should know what is best for the children.

When our children leave for school and other places, do we send them off with a smile and a pleasant farewell?

A child can read a parent's character before he can read the alphabet.

You can't pull the wool over children's eyes, so the best way to teach the Gospel is to live it.

When childhood closes, life's training is mostly done.

Children have only one childhood. We can fail in business and often times start over and make good. But if we fail in the teaching and training of our children, we never get another chance.

To be really effective in training up a child in the way he should go, we must be sure that we travel that road ourselves first.[9]

[9]Joe Wittmer, The Gentle People: Personal Reflections of Amish Life, (Minneapolis, Minnesota: Educational Media Corporation, 1991), 32-35.

Chapter 3
Amish Schooling

The Old Order Amish are staunch in their belief that they do not have any reason to be involved with "English" laws or worldly lifestyle. They live by the Bible, especially the teachings of the Old Testament, and have resisted the pressures of modern society to infringe on their lifestyle and convictions. They choose to be as separate as possible from the rest of the world and all of its problems. They are a closed community, or one in which all family, social, educational and religious activities are conducted within the group. This exclusivity reduces the possibility of the outside world creeping into and eroding their basic doctrines and way of life. In most every facet of their lives they have been able to maintain their separateness. However, education is an area that has caused considerable conflict with secular authorities. The Amish had settled in Pennsylvania during the eighteenth and nineteenth centuries in large numbers. Thaddeus Stevens, a Pennsylvania citizen, was instrumental in providing the basis for the first legislation supporting free public education. That legislation was enacted in 1834 and caused some distress among the Amish communities. The most important teaching in an Amish child's life takes place in the home. There, they are taught the lessons they will need to be a part of the Amish society they were born into. They learn the humility and peace-loving ways that are essential and basic in all Amish persons' lives. They learn the skills needed to be an Amish mother or father. The children learn to be cooperative, selfless and God-fearing from the very earliest stages of their lives. At the preaching services, they learn the lessons of the Old Testament and are taught to be children of God. They really believed that they had no need for the public schools of their English neighbors. But, they soon came to realize that the concept would not pose a threat to their existence and they did send their children to learn the "three R's". By 1930, nearly all Amish children were attending rural one-room public schools and complying with the compulsory education laws of 1925. That legislation required attendance until age fourteen, but local school boards were lenient in permitting absence for necessary farm work and the system was tolerable to the Amish. Also, because the values taught closely mirrored their own and the curriculum supported the agrarian lifestyle they espoused, they were able to go along with some of the changes that occurred over the years. Some of the Amish men even served on the public school boards at that time. But, as the school laws became more and more strict, events occurred which had a significant impact on the education of the Amish children. One Amishman was so outraged by the possibility of the requirement of "excessive education" that he wrote several articles (anonymously) for a Lancaster County, Pennsylvania newspaper. Uncharacteristically, he lashed out at those who wanted compulsory education beyond eighth grade. He said, "Among all the Amish people in Lancaster County, you couldn't find one who ever took any high school, college or vocational school education. Yet I don't believe there's a class of people in the entire world that lead a happier life than do our people on the average. For pity's sake, don't raise the school age for farm children...for if they don't do farm work when they're young they seldom care for it when they're older." He went on, "I am in favor of public schools, but I am not in favor of hiring teachers at twice the salaries that farmers are making to teach our girls to wash dishes and do dance." He described an educated woman whom he knew as, "a bright scholar, a good dancer, busy attending parties, in fact very busy equipping herself to be a modern flapper with lots of pep." He admonished, "Brother, if you want an educated modern wife, I wish you lots of wealth and patience and hope the Lord will have mercy upon your soul." He was a firm believer in experience as the best teacher.[1]

The establishment of the Works Progress Administration (WPA) heralded the end of the one-room schools because of the federal money available for the construction of large school buildings which allowed the consolidation of the small localized districts. In East Lampeter Township in Lancaster County, Pennsylvania, the Amish were very concerned about the federal grant to build a new, large school building and a group of the Amishmen formed An Old Order Amish School Committee consisting of sixteen members and headed by Stephen F. Stoltzfus. They traveled to Washington, D.C. to meet with Harold I. Ickes, the head of the WPA. Mr. Ickes was, understandably, surprised that a group of citizens did not wish to receive the grant and sent them elsewhere to get help. They retained attorneys who were able to get an injunction against the East Lampeter school board and the work on the new building was halted. The U.S. District Court heard the case and that judge ruled in favor of the Amish, basing his decision on their Constitutional rights. However, his ruling was overturned in the U.S. Court of Appeals, the construction was resumed and the school building was finished.[2]

At the same time as the East Lampeter dispute was going on, another threat to the Amish way of life was thrown at them. The legislature passed a law requiring all children to attend school until they were seventeen years old. The school boards' authority to grant exceptions to the attendance regulations was removed and parents of children who did not obey the compulsory attendance law were fined and put in jail. This law was first tested in Chester County, Pennsylvania, near the town of Honey Brook. A girl named Rebecca was kept home from school by her

[1]Intelligencer Journal (Lancaster, Pennsylvania), 19, 20, 21 Feb and 10 Mar 1931.
[2]Gerald S. Lestz, Amish Culture and Society(Ephrata, Pennsylvania: Science Press, 1984), 52.

father in defiance of the new law. Her father was put in jail, but the Amish community was not solidly behind him and his disregard for the civil authorities. The news media picked up the story and immediately dubbed it the "Rebecca of Honey Brook Farm Case." The father appealed through the courts, but was unsuccessful. Although many of them did not agree with the law, many Amish obeyed it, while trying to obtain exceptions and have the law overturned. Farm permits, which allowed the students to stay at home and help with the farm work instead of going to school, were granted at age fifteen, the first year of high school. Two of the ways they tried to avoid sending their children to school beyond age fifteen was to have them do poorly and have to repeat the eighth grade or to keep them home until they were seven years old, which meant that they would be in eighth grade when they reached fifteen and could quit school. They could not be put in high school until they completed that grade and many of them just languished there until they were old enough to get the farm permit. The government tried to deny the permits in an effort to force the Amish children to stay in school until they reached age seventeen. The Amish attitude was,and still is, that the education beyond eighth grade interferes with their religious right to teach their children the fundamentals of their doctrine at home and that schooling beyond age fourteen puts the young people in touch with ideas and concepts they do not need within their own society. They fear that the contact with the worldly concepts would put their youth in jeopardy. They quote this verse from I Cor. 3:19 to explain their aversion to education beyond eighth grade, "...the wisdom of the world is foolishness with God." But, the law stood, through years of litigation, the exceptions were continually denied and the controversy raged on.

After nearly two decades of feuding with public school authorities, spending many nights in jail, imploring the officials to permit them to maintain their own schools, members of the Amish communities in Pennsylvania got some help.

Early in the 1950's, one of the officials of an Amish school in Lancaster County, Noah D. Zook, wrote to the Superintendent of Public Instruction. He asked, "Should not the laws of the state and the rulings of the departments be flexible enough to allow God-fearing people to live their lives and train their children according to the dictates of their conscience?[3] Another official stated the Amish view of education like this, "We are in favor of eight grades of education, but in our way. And our reason for withdrawing at the age of 15 is a religious one. A true Old Order Amish would not send his child to a public high school, regardless of any prosecution."[4] In 1955, Governor George Leader and acting Superintendent of Public Instruction, Ralph C. Swan, persuaded the legislature to reinterpret the school laws and attempt to reach a compromise with the Amish communities. The Amish agreed to comply with fire and safety standards in their school buildings, that their children would attend 180 days of school each year, that their teachers would take the state's high school equivalency tests and that meetings would be held to plan and review the curriculum and other topics that concerned the operation of the Amish schools. Another result was a vocational school system in lieu of high school classes, which allowed Amish young people to use the practical knowledge they gained in their everyday lives as a method of fulfilling the attendance requirement. The program required the students to keep a carefully written journal of their activities and to also attend classes several hours each week. In addition, the teacher would visit the homes of the students to make sure all of the requirements were being met. These vocational schools were to be run by the Amish, attendance records were to be kept, a set group of subjects were to be taught, but the teachers did not have to have certification. [5]

In the meantime, the movement toward Amish parochial

[3]Albert E. Holliday,"The Amish and Compulsory Education,"Pennsylvania Education, January/February 1971, 6.
[4]Ibid.
[5]Ibid., 9.

schools had been progressing slowly. The Amish communities were trying to purchase the one-room schoolhouses that were being abandoned because of the consolidation of so many of the small districts in rural Pennsylvania townships. As they were buying their own buildings, the Amish were providing their own books and supplies and staffing them by hiring retired public school teachers. Because the Amish schools were so far apart and scattered all over the state, there were concerns that the Amish would not adhere to standards. The result was the formation of a statewide committee of Amish school directors. They first met in central Pennsylvania in May of 1957, calling themselves the Parochial School Directors. At the first meeting they exchanged ideas and discussed standardizing the text-books to be used in the schools. As the committee continued to meet annually and become more powerful and involved on the education process, they set teacher's salaries and made policy decisions affecting the schools. They organized the Old Order Book Society from within the committee, which served as a mediator between the directors and the state officials to work out any conflicts between the two. The Old Order Book Society also took on the task of publishing some of the textbooks to be used in the Amish schools. Some Amish teachers had enrolled in correspondence courses. The Society and the bishops frowned on the practice and it was discontinued. When the state raised concern over the use of the heating stoves in the schools, the Society was able to negotiate a solution. A collection method was set up to provide funds for the building of new schools and a limit was set on the cost of a new structure. The issue of singing English rather than German hymns was resolved, as was the celebration of Christmas in schools. Small, modest programs were permitted, but with spiritual focus and without any mention of Santa Claus. The committee continued to meet annually through 1971 and was involved in all facets of Amish education in Pennsylvania.

Other states were also experiencing problems with educating the Amish. In Buchanan, Iowa, during the mid-1960's. There had been a dispute brewing between two local school districts in the area and the Amish school situation provided the catalyst for the two sides to resolve the conflict. The two districts, Hazelton and Oelwein, were attempting a merger, but had opposition from the people in the Hazelton District who wanted no part of a takeover by their rivals in the Oelwein District. The Amish wished to be a part of the adjacent Fairbank Township area which still had one-room schools. They petitioned the officials involved and made their request. However, the Oelwein school officials saw to it that the Amish were turned down because they anticipated losing tax revenues if the Amish children in their district attended private schools. With the merger referendum coming up, the superintendent of the Oelwein district wanted the Amish vote to insure the merger. He persuaded the Amish to vote for the merger, even though their schools were located in the Hazelton district, by promising them they could keep their one-room schools if the merger was approved. The referendum did pass in both districts, overwhelmingly in Oelwein and just barely in Hazelton. When the Hazelton citizenry discovered that the Amish had played such a large part in getting the referendum through, they were outraged. They accused the Amish of using their religion to get what they wanted so they could exploit their children and make fortunes using child labor. They were vehement that the Amish adhere to each and every one of the state's regulations to the letter. A visit by state officials to the Amish schools followed and the two inspectors found the outdoor toilets and stark conditions to be deplorable and ordered changes. The Oelwein board told the Amish they had to agree to the state's requirements and that the board's hands were tied.

For years the Amish communities in Iowa had been trying to meet the state's requirements for certification of teachers. They found it difficult to attract teachers who could earn much higher salaries in the larger consolidated schools and the authorities

43

would often refuse to certify the teachers the Amish were able to hire. The result was that Amish girls were selected to be teachers, based on their natural abilities to relate to children and their aptitude for the subjects to be taught, just as Amish schools in Pennsylvania had done. So, following the state's inspection of their schools, the Amish went back to running their own schools and using Amish girls as teachers.

The disgruntled locals wanted revenge. The Amish were found guilty of breaking the law because of the uncertified teachers and fines were imposed. The Amish refused to pay on the grounds that doing so would be admitting to guilt. So, every day, for several weeks, they were fined $20.00 plus $4.00 in costs. Before too many days passed, the amount owed rose to hundreds and then thousands of dollars. The Amish were threatened with having their farms sold to pay the fines, to no avail. Finally, on November 19, 1965, a group of public school officials entered an Amish school and attempted to force the children to get on their busses and go to the consolidated school. This brought the controversy in Iowa to a head. The news media got wind of the incident and the Amish were in the headlines all over the world.

Iowa's governor, Harold F. Hughes, ordered a three-week cooling-off period and made a visit to the Oelwein school district. The two sides were given a respite, however, when a foundation came forth to pay the salaries of certified teachers in Amish schools for two years. Meanwhile, the fines were paid by anonymous donors and the Amish farms and crops were saved. During the two-year period of compliance, many experts in the field of education studied and expressed opinions about the Amish method of educating their children. The consensus was that the public schools were not a viable alternative for Amish children and that their one-room schools were highly effective in giving them the fundamentals of their religion and providing the basic education needed to exist within their own society. In 1967, the Iowa legislature revised the school code to allow an annual exemption from compliance with its regulations, provided they could prove the competency of their students in certain skill areas.[6] In Maryland and in Ohio, similar changes were made to accommodate the unique Amish situation.

But the conflict between the Amish and the authorities in other states continued. In New Glarus, Wisconsin in 1968, a new community of Old Order Amish was being formed. The fathers of three young people were arrested because they failed to send their children to the local public high school. Two of the young adults, Freida Yoder and Barbara Miller, were fifteen years old and the third, Vernon Yutzy, was fourteen. Each of the children had gone through the eighth grade at the public school, but in Wisconsin, school attendance is compulsory until age sixteen. The Amish do not believe in getting involved in civil matters on their own, so the National Committee For Amish Religious Freedom came to their aid. The group, formed in previous months, hired an attorney and pursued the matter to the Wisconsin Supreme Court. That court found in favor of the Amish, but the Wisconsin Department of Education appealed to the United States Supreme Court, arguing that only state legislatures can decide educational policy, that education is necessary for maintenance of the political system and that the state has the right to free children from ignorance. The high court heard the case and decided, unanimously, in an opinion written by Chief Justice Warren Burger, that "A way of life that is odd or even erratic but interferes with no interests of others is not to be condemned because it is different...However strong is the state's interest in universal compulsory education, it is by no means absolute to the exclusion or subordination of all other interest."[7]

The main witness for the Amish was Dr. John Hostetler, an authority who is well-known among the Amish. His comments on the case follow:

---

[6]John A. Hostetler, <u>Amish Society</u> (Baltimore: Johns Hopkins University Press, 1980), 258-262.
[7]<u>Wisconsin v. Yoder et al.</u>, U. S. Supreme Court. No. 70-110. Argued December 8, 1971; decided may 15, 1972.

45

"The decision of the Supreme Court, upholding the right of the Amish to train their own children on completing eight years of schooling, finally puts an end to the years of harassment the Amish have suffered in one state or another.

No longer must they choose between criminal sanctions on the one hand and abandoning their religious practices and view of education, which sustains their community, on the other.

This landmark decision will force many educators to take a fresh look at the education of minority groups. Something has been seriously wrong with our public policy and the education of our minority groups. At issue was not learning the basic skills, but basic values.

When culturally different children attend a school that teaches an unattainable identity, an identity that would demand a rejection of the values of the home, of the parents, the tribe, or the street, even the color of their skin, what can be expected but alienation and rebellion?

Public policy in this country has operated on the melting pot theory--molding immigrant people to be exactly like one another--thus obliterating cultural differences. With the Supreme Court decision, there is now protection against the coercive powers of the state to obliterate cultural differences of no harm to anyone.

Whether or not one is sympathetic to the Amish position, there are some lessons we can learn from them. They are keenly aware of the destructive influence of technology on their community and on their land. They have shunned certain aspects of technology, preferring to take the paths of wisdom. Our public schools have stressed technology. We have more than enough technologically competent barbarians. We need both technology and wisdom, and in a manner that is socially acceptable and socially responsible.

This decision does not excuse the Amish from compulsory education. The Amish have devised one of the most effective systems of vocational education for their way of life. A recent study of their education that I completed shows that:

1. Half of the Amish in this country are in public schools in rural areas. They form private schools only when they are forced into a school environment where they must choose between being Amish or being American. They want to be both.

2. There were 16 Amish schools in 1950. Today there are over 300 with an estimated enrollment of 10,000 pupils.

3. Amish pupils score higher than pupils in public schools in the basic skills, arithmetic, spelling and word usage.

4. Theirs is a school without walls, where children become competent by vocational training in the farm and domestic tasks required by their culture. They learn to do by doing.

5. Single-handed, the Amish communities raise their children to thrive on cooperation, humility and a fear of God, rather than competition and the pride of intellect.

6. The Amish young aspire to become adults and follow the occupation of their parents. Those who want to, leave their society and readily assimilate into the larger society."[8]

Although there have been no major educational upheavals or

[8]Lestz, ibid., 67.

head-to-head confrontations with the authorities for the Amish during the past two decades, there has been some internal disagreement. Even with the Supreme Court's landmark ruling in 1972, some Amish parents are anxious to send their children to public schools so that they might have contact with English children at an early age. On the opposite side of that debate are those parents who wish to keep their children as separate as possible from the worldly influences found in the public schools. However, most of the Amish children today are enrolled in a one-room private school run by their parents and staffed by a young Amish girl with only an eighth grade education. The decision is largely a personal one, though, and has not caused so much unrest that the bishops and other church officials have had to intervene.

To step into an Amish one-room schoolhouse is to step a century or more back in time. There are neat rows of old-fashioned wooden desks, the teacher's desk is at the front of the room and the wood or coal-burning stove, the only source of heat, is at the center of the room. There is a cloakroom, or a row of hooks or pegs for coats and hats along the wall on one side of the room and a battery-operated clock hangs on the wall above the blackboard. Also above the board are large cards with the letters of the English alphabet, written in script. Just below each of them is the corresponding letter of the German alphabet, in old German lettering. Because there are no electric lights, the windows are quite large to allow as much natural light in as possible. There are kerosene lanterns hanging at regular intervals from the low ceiling, as a supplemental light source. Along one side of the room is the recitation desk or bench, where students repeat their sums, or their spelling, as a group. The restroom facilities are out behind the schoolhouse. There are two outhouses or "privies", one for the boys and one for the girls.

The typical Amish school day begins at 8:30 a.m. with roll call. The Amish children are present unless they are ill. Average attendance is higher than that in public schools because the whole school is closed for peak planting and harvest times when the children are needed at home. The other days off are few and far between, with only a very brief one or two day break at Christmas and none for the other holidays. The day is divided into four blocks of teaching time with a 15 minute recess between the two morning and afternoon sessions. There is also a lunch break of one-half hour in the middle of the day. Following roll call, all of the children take part in devotions. The scripture is read in German and the Lord's Prayer is recited in unison, also in German. Because German is the only language they have heard in the home, many of the young children are exposed to spoken and written English for the first time when they attend school. All of the lessons are taught in English except for the German scripture and prayers. The Amish parents are well aware that their children must be able to interact and communicate with the English-speaking world as adults. As the first lessons get underway, the children are given a few minutes to review the previous day's work. The classes take their turn at the recitation desk to let the teacher know what they have accomplished. The students recite as a group, with no special recognition for anyone. There is none of the competition for grades or attention that is found in the public schools. As each group recites, the others are working on their lessons at their seats. The subjects taught are math, including addition, subtraction, multiplication, division, volume and area, decimals and percentages, weights and measures and interest, which is considered to be very important and necessary in managing the Amish household and farm accounts; reading, in English, which most of the children enjoy; writing, also in English, including grammar, spelling, and composition; history; geography; health and nature study. Science, as such is avoided because of the technology involved and religion is not formally taught because it is so emphasized in all phases of an Amish person's life. Further, the Amish feel that only ordained persons should interpret and explain the scriptures for the group. The school board selects the textbooks, using the recommendations of the statewide committee and, sometimes, with the teacher's input. There is a list of appropriate textbooks put out by the Old Order Book Society. Sometimes, public schools donate discarded textbook which are welcomed by the Amish for use in their schools. The older books are preferred because sex education, advanced science and technology are not discussed. Many of the books used are published by Pathway Publishers, of Aylmer, Ontario, Canada and LaGrange, Indiana, which the Amish own and operate. They also publish *Blackboard Bulletin*, a monthly newsletter for teachers. They prefer works written by Amish authors and two of the widely used histories are, Seeking A Better Country, by Noah Zook and Our Better Country: The Story of America's Freedom, by Uria, R. Byler.

At recesses and during the noontime break, the children head for the playground and the ballfield where games of tag, jumping rope, blindman's bluff, and softball take place. Some of the games played by Amish children are reminiscent of the games played by school children a century or more ago. One favorite is corner ball, which is an outdoor game played on a field measuring any where from 20' by 30' to 30' by 60'. A large ball is needed. A basketball, volleyball or similarly sized playball will work just fine. The bases are on each corner and are four or five feet square and there is a line across the center of the field. There are seven players on a team. Two of them man the two corner bases of the opposing team, two more are guards and the remaining three are tossers. A coin toss decides first possession. The tossers attempt to get the ball to one of their basemen by throwing, rolling or bouncing it through the opposing team members. The basemen must have one foot on the base when catching the ball and the guards commit a foul if they stray inside the bases. A foul is also committed by anyone who touches the ball while an opponent is touching it. Points are scored every time a baseman catches the ball inside the designated square, The game is played for two, ten minute halves.

There are usually sliding boards and swings on the playground and a nearby hillside for sledding in the winter. Another old-fashioned game which is played in the winter is fox and geese or wheel tag. One or more large circle paths, one outside the other, are cleared on a snow-covered flat field. Then the "spokes" of the wheel, usually just four of them, are cleared and the center, or hub, is the goal, or safe spot. This game can also be played when there is no snow covering the ground by using lime to mark the paths. One player is the fox, and chases the others (the geese) and tries to tag them. No one is permitted to run outside of the path and that infraction results in making the offender the fox. The geese are permitted to jump from one path to another, but the fox may not, nor is he permitted to tag a goose across a path. A goose may remain safe while standing in the center, but only one goose at a time is allow to occupy that spot. When a new goose reaches the spot, the first one must leave.

The children are all involved in the games, a spirit of cooperation and fairplay prevails and nobody is ever left out, including the teacher, who always takes part in the fun. The children all bring their lunches and enjoy the homemade sandwiches and cookies, cakes, pies and other goodies hurriedly so they can get to the games. On many school playgrounds the children converse in both English and German. The language to be used during playtimes is decided by the parents and the bishop.

The Amish school day ends at 3:30 p.m. after a short time of all classes singing together. But, they do not leave immediately. They must sweep out the schoolroom, empty wastebaskets, clean the blackboards and erasers, line the desks up in a neat row and put the books and other teaching materials away. In cold weather, when a fire is needed to heat the room, someone must restock the wood box or coal bucket and bank the fire for the following day. Only then, when all the janitorial chores are finished, do the children put on their hats, pick up their lunch pails and head for home.

Discipline is not really a problem in Amish schools because

the children are trained from a very early age to be submissive and to obey. In those cases where it becomes necessary to punish a child in school, the teacher is the ultimate authority. Unlike the public school teachers in most districts, the Amish teacher has permission, or, rather, the duty, to use corporal punishment. The following essay on the subject was written by Uria R. Byler and puts the topic in perspective from the Amish point of view:

As one who helped to raise a family, I have found that one of life's most tasteless tasks is to spank your child. However hard that may be, it is much more so if you punish someone else's child, and I don't believe the teacher lives who does not dread that thankless task. It should be used only as a last resort, after all other methods have been tried and have failed.

The teachers in the Amish school are very fortunate that they have the right to apply the rod if necessary. The parents usually do not resent this, and the great majority will cooperate with the teacher. The few who do not, and who look unkindly on this practice if their children are involved, are only doing harm to themselves, and to their children, besides making it miserable for the teacher.

We have heard it said quite often by teachers that a child's home life, or environment, is mirrored by his actions at school. Very true. A teacher does not have to be a wizard or a magician to figure it out. Here is a never-failing test to decide whether little Johnny is under proper discipline at home...watch his reactions when he gets punished, however lightly, for breaking school rules.

We'll say Johnny decides to do his spelling the easy way, he cheats. Due punishment is administered. If he is the friendly little chap as before, then it is a good guess that he is behaving at home, and used to being punished if he is not. But if he pouts for a few days, then you may be quite sure that he does not like to be under any authority, simply because it's something new to him, and that he probably has his own way at home.

It is conceded by many noted educators in public schools that a great thing was lost when they took the rod away from the teachers.[9]

Reading is a popular pastime among the Old Order Amish, and in some areas with large Amish populations, the local public library's bookmobiles serve the Amish schools and community. One such area is in Holmes County, Ohio, where the county public library system sends its mobile library into the countryside to provide library service that would not be readily available otherwise. Most of the stops are at Amish schools but there are other established points, such as a general store or a public park where the bookmobile stops regularly. Many of the patrons are the school children, but there is also a sizeable contingent of Amish women who await the bookmobile's arrival. The Amish men make up the fewest number of patrons who use the service. The women usually borrow religious or inspirational fiction, while the children tend to favor animal stories, books about pioneer life and those with western or cowboy themes. One of the biggest problems facing the library staff is the shortage of the kinds of books preferred by the Amish readers. Many of the old editions of the classics and works by their favorite authors are out of print and impossible to find. They are fond of books by Danny Orliss, Thomas E. Hinkle, Stephen Meade, and Edward Dolch. The series they most want to read are about Five Yard Fuller, Jim Forrest, Happy Hollister, Dan Frontier and Cowboy Sam and Shorty. The copies owned by the library are in terrible

[9]Uria R. Byler, "What About Corporal Punishment?" Blackboard Bulletin, February, 1963, in John A. Hostetler, Editor, Amish Roots: A Treasury of History, Wisdom and Lore, (Baltimore: The Johns Hopkins University Press, 1989), 113-114.

condition and have been mended and re-mended to keep them in circulation. But the Amish bookmobile patrons want to read them, no matter what condition they are in.[10]

---

[10]Gayle Patton, "Plain and Simple Pleasures: Bookmobile Service in Amish Country", Wilson Library Bulletin, March 1994.

Chapter 4
Courtship and Marriage

Courtship in the Old Order Amish culture takes place at about the same time as *Rum springa*, after the young adults are finished with their eight years of school and are preparing for adulthood and all its responsibilities. The Amish must marry only within their own group and even then, marrying someone from a more liberal Amish church district is frowned upon and forbidden by some bishops. Because of the limitations of horse and buggy travel, most Amish do end up marrying someone from their own church district. Although intermarriage could pose a problem in a culture which is so isolated and separate from other groups, the church leaders have forbidden marriage between first cousins. Second cousin marriages are discouraged, but do happen occasionally. In Lancaster County, Pennsylvania it is also taboo to marry a "Swartz cousin", so named because Jacob Swartz married Magdelena Stoltzfus (b. June 18, 1832). She was his "first cousin once removed" (the child of his first cousin). Swartz was excommunicated.[1]

The courtship ritual is a fairly standard one among the Amish and is done in secrecy as far as is possible. One of the most important social activities for the adolescents is a Sunday evening singing. On the evening after the preaching service, which is held on alternate Sundays, the young people gather at the home which hosted the earlier worship service. They are all dressed

---

[1]John A. Hostetler, <u>Amish Society</u>, (Baltimore: The Johns Hopkins University Press,1981), 148.

in their very best clothes and the horse and buggy are also "shined up" for the evening. Although the singing is for the purpose of pairing off the young people, the boy does not usually pick up his favorite girl and take her to the singing. He will take his sisters and, perhaps, her friends, but will find his *Madel* or date, later. The young people who gather are usually from several different church districts which provides a wider range of prospective mates for the young people. This is not considered a worship service, but, rather, is purely social. The young adults are seated at long tables, boys on one side and girls at the other. Only the single young people who have not been baptized participate in the singing. They take turns leading the songs, or taking the role of the *Vorsinger*, the one who chooses the song and begins the first note to set the pitch. Only the faster hymns from the <u>Ausbund</u>, the Amish hymnal which was first printed in 1564, are sung, rather than the slower ones that are used at the preaching service, and there is never any musical accompaniment. There is a break between each song and lighthearted conversations take place at that time. It is during these breaks that many of the boys will seek out their dates and ask to give them a ride home. At about 10 p.m. the singing is over and the young people have a snack and talk among themselves and enjoy each other's company. Any of the boys who do not already have a date for the rest of the evening choose a girl during this social time. Although it is not condoned by the parents and church leaders, there is sometimes dancing after the singing. If there are guitars, harmonicas or other of the forbidden musical instruments hidden nearby, they are brought out and the more lively fun begins as the crowd adjourns to the barn for the dancing. Even though these dances are not permitted, members of the older generation turn their heads and silently hope that the adolescents will come to their senses. Alcohol is occasionally brought into these dances and is, of course absolutely forbidden to those who have been baptized.

Following the singing and the dancing, the young couples

hitch up the horses and make their way home under the stars. Although the Amish lifestyle is a serene one on the surface, these young adults are given much freedom at this stage of their lives and are often out courting most of the night, which is acceptable in their culture.

The ones who have paired off do not ever refer to each other by name, but use personal pronouns, instead. The boy is called a *beau* or *Kal* or "fellow" and the courting process is referred to as dating. The couples are most secretive about their relationship and do everything they can to keep the whole thing concealed. The only time they are publicly together as a couple is when leaving the singing or barn dance. If the word gets out that a couple are courting, then a great deal of kidding must be endured by the pair.

There are other kinds of social occasions when the adolescents may mingle and get to know one another. Things like auctions, husking bees, frolics (work sessions) and family visits provide some social interaction, but these are usually held close to home so there is little chance of meeting anyone new. There is a widely held myth among the "English" that a blue gate or front door at an Amish home signifies that there are unmarried, available daughters. There is no research to support such a folksy idea and it is just one of those stories that is so widely circulated that no one is really sure of its origin. When asked if the large number of blue gates and doors found in one western Pennsylvania Amish community meant that there was a bumper crop of available young women, one Amish women replied, "No, that is just our favorite color to paint gates and doors."

If a couple is courting, then they will also spend alternate Saturday nights together on weeks when there is no preaching service scheduled for the next day. He will dress in his Sunday best, again, and make sure the horse and buggy are cleaned up and make little or no mention to his family of his destination. He will act very casually and try to give everyone the impression that he is headed for town on business. He must make sure he arrives at his steady girl's house after the parents and grandparents have gone to bed for the night. He alerts her that he is there by shining a flashlight beam on her window. That is her signal that she should come and let him in. The couple will either spend their time together in the sitting room of the house or will go upstairs to the girl's bed where they will spend most of the night lying there together...fully clothed and just talking. This practice is known as "bundling", or *Bei-schlof* (with sleep) and is not necessarily looked upon with approval by all Old Order Amish bishops.

Bundling, or "tarrying", as it is also called, has its origin in the British Isles and Europe as well as in the Orient, and is not exclusively an Amish custom. The very practical consideration for bundling is as a wood-saving measure. In the days when everyone heated with wood, the families went to bed early, after carefully banking the fire to preserve the embers for morning. A young couple courting would be quite chilly if the fire was banked for the night and their wooing was done in the parlor or living room. Thus, the custom of going to the girl's bed to lie down under the covers, while fully dressed, resulted. There have always been those who opposed the practice, as well as those who thought it was a sensible idea. The following is the opinion of A. Monroe Aurand, Jr., who was active in the 1930's and 1940's as an author and observer of customs and social life:

> Many declared it (bundling) was the means of bringing them into close harmony with chaste young women, eventually ending in a happy and fruitful marriage.
>
> If there is anything that "makes" a man want to be friendly with the rest of the world, it is when he sees an innocent young couple engaged in the hand-in-hand type of courtship.
>
> This feeling is even increased when we see what transpires on the park benches, and in the parks, on the porch-swings, and in the automo-

bile; even the theatre balcony, or dark recesses, reveal the emotion of lovers; the decks of ferry-boats and the corridors of great office buildings are not without evidence of courtship and its many allies.

Bundling has its evolution, and unless one is well versed in this lore, one fails to recognize some of our most modern courting arrangements as a part of the scheme of things first instituted in the ages long ago, and generally authorized by the well-known Naomi, mother-in-law of Ruth, who married Boaz after a novel bundling adventure...in Ruth, Chapter 3, verses 6 and 13.

Naturally there will be two sides to the question, as to whether bundling, as a custom in the New World, is good, or bad.

Let us say that where the intent of young people to court in bed is entirely honest, we subscribe to the theory that it cannot be morally wrong. Gentlemen can be gentlemen at all times, and ladies can be ladies, as long as they want to, short of violence.

Even under the present system of judging others by their own selfish desires and longings, we do not anticipate that every bundling couple is going to violate the bounds of decency and morality.

It is a common human weakness to judge others by all the evil things we can conjure in our minds, to deprive others of what, deep down in our hearts we could relish with the greatest of satisfaction (and we secretly wish we could, perhaps, endure).

In several brief installments in "The Herald of Truth" (an official publication of the Old Order

Amish Mennonite Church) bundling is discussed by one who would even go so far as to tell the bishops, and ministers, that the old custom is "wrong," even if they personally indulged in it in their youth--and by their indifference (or sense of caution) still encourage it today.

Traditionally we suppose that bundling in bed would be about the extent of "prohibition" suggested to a layman, but see to what lengths this writer goes:

"Today it seems to be the most popular practice among the young sisters of our Amish Mennonite churches to disregard, remove, and lay aside the devotional head covering during courting. WHY? Of course we all know that it is wrong for a young woman to pray with her head uncovered. But, you may ask, why would it be wrong for her to "entertain" her boyfriend with her head uncovered? Perhaps you will say you neither pray nor prophesy when he is there. If that is the case-- young brother, you'd be safer at home.

During those courting hours time is not all taken up in conversation...what are we thinking during those silent moments?...When we forget to even thank God; to consider whether he is pleased or grieved; yea, when courtship (?) is indulged just for **silly fun**; and when we trust our own strength against the craftiness of the devil, those silent moments might be **dangerous**. For a child of God, who engages in courtship, it is very essential and necessary to pray...(hence the need to wear the head covering!)

If the way in which many (yea, alas! too many) courtships among the Amish young people are conducted, were made known to the public!...There are those of other denominations who highly esteemed and respected the Amish Church, but when they learned of our, we must admit, lowdown standard of courtship were utterly shocked...

In the first place, it is greatly to be feared that a large percentage of the popularly so-called "dates" among us Amish young people of today, are only "dates" and no real courtship whatsoever. Is it not sadly true that of many, many "dates" the motive is not honest, true, sincere, pure and careful Christian love? But an unholy lusty "necking" (as it has been termed by many and rightly so). This is an ungodly motive...

Where is there a **modest** brother or sister who could without shame confess the **practice of bed courtship?** This term includes not only **"under the cover"** but **on top of the cover, as well**...Why is bed courtship wrong?....Anyone with ordinary mental ability very well knows that the Devotional Covering and bed courtship do not go well together...the Covering denotes (or at least it should) modesty, respect, chastity, purity, subjection, and obedience; while bed courtship readily indicates immodesty, immorality, unchasteness, carelessness, impudence, indecency, shamelessness, lack of respect for one another, lack of self-respect.

Of course we know and realize that our opponents on this subject are not all young folks and lay members, but we frankly admit, and this is with some shame, that there are even some ministers and bishops among our denomination who seek to justify this. Some say, "*Es is der alt Gebrauch,*" and "*Es is die alt Ordnung,*" (meaning, "it is the old need or custom or order").

It has also been said in regard to **courting in a sitting position,** "*Es fiihrt in der Hochmuth,*" (it leads to pride)...The commonly approved type of courtship may be equal with that of the world; **but bundling is lower than that**...because bed courtship is **different** by no means makes it better, more respectable, more modest, or more pleasing to God.

When we were little boys and girls, and as we entered the early teen-age years we used to wonder how young folks conducted courtship...**that when we learned of bed courtship, we were greatly shocked... How did we** (the writer included) **ever get to the point that we became guilty of this practice?...**"[2]

The addition of central heating systems in modern homes has made the practice disappear from "English" society. There is, however, much debate among outsiders concerning whether or not bundling is still done in Amish society. Because the Amish are so private and feel that their courting rituals are nobody else's business, there is really no way of knowing. But, the Amish as a whole probably do not any longer use bundling as a courtship method, but there is reason to believe that it is still practiced in some of the church districts, depending upon how liberal the leadership is. Whatever the style of courtship in Amish society,

---

[2]A. Monroe Aurand, Jr., Little Known Facts About Bundling in the New World, (Lancaster, Pennsylvania: The Aurand Press, n.d.), 16.

premarital sex is strictly forbidden, as is any form of birth control. Although there are no statistics available on the number of premarital pregnancies that occur among the Amish, it would seem logical that the number is less than in the rest of society. There are very rarely cases of unwed Amish mothers and the couples who do make the mistake of engaging in premarital sex and find themselves expecting a child are said to "have to join church," rather than "have to get married," as the expression goes among the "English." The couple is punished by the church, as is demanded by the *Ordnung*, and *Meidung*, or "shunning" is imposed until a full confession has been made and the pair has asked the congregation for forgiveness. When this has been accomplished, there will be a wedding and there is no shame or stigma attached to the event as there is in "English" society.

There is no formal sex education in the Amish culture. It is just not spoken of and the children keep their questions to themselves, even when they observe the normal mating activities of the farm animals. They, like children in all other cultures, talk among themselves about the topic, but there is never an opportunity to formally receive such information. As a result, many young Amish couples reach their marriage bed without a clue as to what happens next.

When a couple does decide to get married, they have made the decision to put aside the trappings and freedom of youth and settle down to the business of church membership, adulthood, responsibility and raising a family. The young man informs a minister or deacon, who will be his *Schtecklimann*, or middle man. This go-between visits the girl's home and asks the parents for their permission for the marriage. The groom's spokesman then tells the bishop about the couple's plans and the bishop makes the appropriate announcement in church. (If the couple belong to different congregations, the deacon of the groom's church brings a letter of good standing to the deacon of the bride's congregation and he also meets with her parents to confirm their approval. The deacon from the bride's church then "publishes" the plans to her congregation.) On that day, the prospective bride does not attend the preaching service, but stays at her home and awaits her fiance's visit. The bridegroom attends church and when the announcement of his wedding is made, he leaves the service to go to his fiancee's home to tell her that the bishop has made the public revelation. The community is not to know of the event until it is "published", or announced, in church, two Sundays before the wedding day. After the announcement of the intentions of the couple, the fellow moves into the girl's house to help with all the many preparations for their big day. Engagement, as such, is not known among the Amish, but some other signs are evident. These may be an especially large amount of celery in the bride's family's garden, because of the great amount of celery used at the wedding feast. Another clue is an Amish bridegroom's father's search for an extra farm for the newlyweds or his remodeling of a vacant house on his farm.[3]

Most Amish weddings are held in November or December, after the hard work of harvesting the crops and preparing for winter are done. The ceremony always take place on a Tuesday or a Thursday, in the home of the bride. No formal, written invitations are issued. It is the groom's duty to personally invite all of his relatives. If there are relatives who live too far away to be invited personally, then postcards are mailed to them. The aunts and uncles and close friends of the couple are issued special invitations to serve as cooks and overseers. It is a special honor to be asked to assist the couple in this way. The parents of the couple make the final decision about the servers and, although they have much hard work to do in preparation for the wedding, they do not do any of the work on the wedding day. There are variations in the details of the marriage customs from one church community to another and from one geographical location to another. The wedding guests, which may number

---

[3]Hostetler, 148.

from 40-600, are served both a midday meal and an evening meal. The quantities prepared are enormous, and the noon feast, alone, for a typical wedding, requires:

80 fryers

8 stewing hens to make 2 canners (7 gallons) of chicken gravy

12-14 gallons peeled potatoes

20-30 loaves of homemade bread for dressing

24 lbs. frozen peas

4 gallons gelatin with fruit and whipped cream topping added

5 gallons cole slaw with onion, celery, carrot and red pepper

15 layer cakes beside the Bridal cake)

2 three pound cans of coffee

1 regular size jar instant coffee

30 lb. cheese and 50 lbs. cold ham to pass

A modern wedding supper requires:

65 lbs. hamburger for meatloaf

4 gallons cooked and diced potatoes for salad

12 lbs. dry noodles to make 2 large canners full

8 batches of date pudding with sauce

12 apple and 12 cherry pies to be served with ice cream

Wedding punch is also served and is made from:

1 46 oz. can orange juice

1 46 oz. can pineapple juice

1 46 oz. can grapefruit juice

1 12 oz. can frozen lemonade

1 qt. gingerale

Keep all on ice until just before serving and serve over ice cubes.[4]

The description that follows is of a wedding in central Pennsylvania, from the observations of John A. Hostetler.

Food preparations began the day before the

---

[4]Emma Byler, Plain and Happy Living: Amish Recipes and Remedies, (Cleveland, Ohio: Goosefoot Acres Press, 1991), 58-60.

wedding. The cooks, thirty or more, and all married couples, started arriving at the bride's home before 7 a.m. According to custom, the bridegroom chopped off the heads of all the fowl and the men picked the feathers from the chickens, ducks and turkeys. The women washed them, prepared the dressing and stuffed them, then washed dishes, baked many, many pies, peeled two bushels of potatoes and cracked walnuts and hickory nuts. Meanwhile, the men cleaned the celery, kept up with the large demand for hot water, emptied the garbage and built the temporary tables to be placed in the main rooms of the house for the wedding feast. Six pine tables and benches were set up on three of the outside walls of the livingroom, and in the bedroom, as well as in the kitchen. The seating capacity was 100. The chickens, ducks and turkeys, all dressed and stuffed, were put into large outdoor ovens the evening before the wedding.

The wedding day is a day of great celebration and fun for all the family and guests, but, especially for the young people. Before the sun came up on their wedding day, the bride and groom, dressed in new, but typical "Sunday" clothes, along with the two couples who were their attendants, went to a neighbor's home which was the site of the preaching service and wedding. They were on their way to a service, which everyone was invited to, but was attended mainly by the wedding guests.

By 9 a.m. the guests had arrived for the ceremony and preaching service. The bride and groom were seated in the front seat before the guests arrived. As the service began, with singing, the ministers adjourned to the council room, followed by the couple. As the congregation sang wedding hymns from the *Ausbund*, the ministers counseled the couple on the duties of marriage. The bride and groom returned to the congregation, holding hands, and took their seats near the ministers.

The bishop delivered the main sermon about marriages in the Old Testament: the story of Adam and Eve; the wickedness of mankind after the flood, in the foolishness of the wives they had chosen; the uprightness of Noah's household in not intermarrying with unbelievers; the story of Isaac and Rebecca, and the adulterous plight of Solomon. The bishop ended his sermon with a retelling from the Apocrypha, Tobit, Chapters 1-14, about how Tobias was careful to obey his father's instructions in finding a wife from his own tribe in spite of major difficulties.

Around noon, after the long sermon was over, the bishop summoned the couple. The marriage ceremony was about to begin. It was carried out without written text and consisted of several questions and answers, and concluded with the bishop placing his hands on the clasped hands of the couple.

The vows, which are repeated in German, are:

"You have now heard the ordinance of Christian wedlock presented. Are you now willing to enter wedlock together as God in the beginning ordained and commanded?

Yes.

Do you stand in the confidence that this, our sister, is ordained of God to be your wedded wife?

Yes.

Do you stand in the confidence that this, our

brother is ordained of God to be your wedded husband?

Yes.

Do you also promise your wedded wife, before the Lord and His church, that you will nevermore depart from her, but will care for her and cherish her, if bodily sickness comes to her, or in any circumstance which a Christian husband is responsible to care for, until the dear God will again separate you from each other?

Yes.

Do you also promise your wedded husband, before the Lord and his church, that you will nevermore depart from him, but will care for him and cherish him, if bodily sickness comes to him, or in any circumstance which a Christian wife is responsible to care for, until the dear God will again separate you from each other?

Yes."

The couple joined their right hands as the bishop went on: "So then may I say with Raguel (Tobit 7:15), the God of Abraham the God of Isaac and the God of Jacob be with you and help you together and fulfill his blessing abundantly upon you, through Jesus Christ, Amen."

Near the end of the ceremony the servers and several relatives slipped out of the house to make last minute preparations for the wedding meal. The closing formalities lasted another half hour. Then the newly married couple and their attendants walked to the buggies parked at the end of the yard. The hostlers were ready to drive the couples to the bride's home, and did so while sitting on the laps of the couples!

There were no shouts or hoots or handshakes

or claps on the back as they reached their destination. The couples quietly and without any sort of response from the wedding guests, went directly to an upstairs bedroom, along with their attendants. (This was all done in a most somber mood, and, contrary to the legend, the young men did not throw the groom over the fence for luck.) Meanwhile, the bride's father was busy seating the guests in order of kinship. The bridal table or *Eck* (corner table) had been placed in the most visible part of the livingroom. When they returned, the groom sat on the right of the bride with attendants on each side. The unmarried girls sat with their backs to the wall around the bridal table and the unmarried young men sat across from the girls. Married couples sat similarly at the other tables. Opposite the newlyweds was the *Schnutzler* (carver) who would carve the fowl for the *Eck* and make sure the wedding party was well served.

As soon as all the seats were full, the bishop gave the signal for silent prayer. Then the feasting began. There were roast ducks, chickens and turkeys and dressing, mashed potatoes, gravy, cold ham, cole slaw, raw and cooked celery, peaches, prunes, pickles, bread and butter, jams, cherry pie, tea, cookies and many kinds of cake. The guests ate heartily and visited. As soon as the first group of 100 guests were finished, the tables were cleared, the dishes hastily washed and dried, and the tables were reset. The second group of guests were seated and the feasting went on. This was done once more to accommodate all of the guests and the bridal party remained at their seats until all of the guests had eaten.

Then the time came for singing. One of the

Vorsingers announced the hymn and all joined in except the bridal couple. It is considered a bad omen for them to sing at their own wedding. Women do not normally lead the singing, but at a wedding the women frequently take that role. As the afternoon wore on the young people left the tables to go out to the yard or the barn to continue their visiting until time for the wedding supper.

At the supper, all the unmarried young people are required to sit in couples. If a boy had a "steady" then he had no problem finding a partner, but those who had no special girl or were inexperienced in the dating ritual were hard pressed to ask a girl to join them. If a young man refused to find his own partner, then he was forcibly dragged to the door and paired with a girl. The couples then entered the house, hand in hand, and found their places at the tables. The wedding supper consisted of roast beef, roast chicken, noodles, beef gravy, chicken gravy, mashed potatoes, cole slaw, prunes, fruit salad, potato chips, cookies, pies, cakes and, for the bridal party and the cooks, there were baked oysters and ice cream. There was singing throughout the wedding supper, which lasted until about 10 p.m. During the evening from special plates of goodies were sent from the *Eck* to the closest friends of the couple. The supper ended with the singing of *Guter Geselle* (good friend), a religious folk song. This song is not found in any Amish songbooks and is sung from memory. The last verse is:

> Good friend, what do you say?
> O good friend I tell you--
> I tell you what one thing is:
> One is God alone.

He who lives and He who soars,
And He who leads the true Faith
In Heaven and on Earth.

The young people again left the tables to go to the barn for games and the married couples returned to their homes. The cooks stayed on to finish the cleaning up and take care of the left over food.

The parents of the couple were not at the ceremony, nor did they receive any special recognition during the festivities. They were kept busy seeing that the cooking and serving were going well and even ate with the cooks and servers. The bride and groom were treated with great respect as they sat at the *Eck* and the entire celebration was for their enjoyment. When they left the bridal table, however, they were treated just as everyone else. Still, there were no special expressions of congratulations or good luck. This is apparently taken for granted.[5]

The couple spent their wedding night at the bride's parent's home and there is no honeymoon in the Amish culture. The couple is expected to spend the next few weeks traveling to the homes of aunts and uncles and collecting wedding gifts as they go from house to house. Prior to the wedding, both families set about gathering items for the couple's dowry. The things in the dowry are for the purpose of helping them set up housekeeping and are often homemade things and crafts. The wedding guests are also expected to bring a gift to the wedding and these gifts run the gamut of household items. They are displayed on the bed in an upstairs bedroom at the bride's home and include dishes, kerosene lamps, bedspreads, blankets, tablecloths, towels,

---

[5]Hostetler, 191.

clocks, handkerchiefs and small farm tools. The parents of the couple provide furniture and livestock and, sometimes, basic equipment. In addition, all Amish mothers start years in advance to make quilts for each of their children, to be given to them when they establish their own homes. One woman made three quilts and two comforters for each of her seven boys and three girls![6]

The Amish truly marry for life and divorce is forbidden. They have been reared all their lives to become baptized in the church, choose a suitable mate and accept the responsibilities of marriage and adulthood. The couple is a welcome addition to the community because they will provide another home for the preaching services to be held and will continue the tradition of raising a large family.

---

[6]Hostetler, 151.

Chapter 5
Amish Farming and Trades

To the Old Order Amish working with the soil is a Christian's obligation. As spelled out in Genesis 2:15, "And the Lord God took the man and put him into the Garden of Eden to dress it and keep it," man is expected to be a steward of the land and is responsible for maintaining it and nurturing it. The land is precious and fragile and man has been trusted to treat it well and not destroy it. The Amish are a hard-working and orderly people and working with the soil has always fit perfectly into their basic religious philosophy. Their Anabaptist ancestors in Switzerland and the Palatinate were agrarian and were well-known for their ability as farmers. During the eighteenth century, early in their history, when their persecuted ancestors fled the Alsace region of France to search for religious freedom, the French officials were keenly aware of the economic impact they had made upon the area. They "apply themselves with extraordinary care to the agriculture, an occupation for which they have an admirable knowledge. They transformed the sterile and dry lands into tillable lands and the most beautiful pastures of the province."[1] Even though they were not permitted to own land, they rented acreage and cleared the land to make pastures, orchards, gardens and fields for their crops. They were known as the most

---

[1]Jean Seguy, "Religion and Agricultural Success: The Vocational life of the French Anabaptists from the Seventh to the Nineteenth Centuries," Trans. Michael Shank, _Mennonite Quarterly Review_, 47 (July 1973): 182.

diligent workers and all the members of the family worked from dawn until after nightfall to make a success of their lives. Several generations were found in one household, working together for the good of all. As the parents aged, the next generation would frequently take over and assume the majority of the farm work, allowing the older generation to enjoy an early retirement amid the family unit. Because they had long-term leases, there was added incentive for improving the land and developing innovative farming methods. They were among the first to rotate crops using a three-year system that had wheat planted the first year; rye, barley and clover during the second year and potatoes, carrots and turnips for the third year of the sequence. They were also the first to use manure from their cattle to fertilize the fields and to use other forms of mineral fertilizers. They found and mined gypsum, developed a way to process it in kilns and put it on their fields.[2] When they crossed the Atlantic to make their new homes in America, they brought their love of the soil and talent for farming with them. The fertile limestone soil in Lancaster County, Pennsylvania was especially suited to their lifestyle and willingness to work longer and harder than their neighbors. One diary of an early Pennsylvania settler describes the efforts of David Mast (1798-1869), an Amish deacon and experimental farmer whose unique use of ground bone as a means of restoring phosphorus and potassium to the soils became widely used.

> September 12, 1845: This David Mast is one of the most enterprising men of our neighborhood and as an agriculturist he has scarcely his equal. To the knowledge of his various theories he adds an extensive practice and is not too timid to indulge in experiments.

> October 15, 1845: David Mast proposes manuring the Watts farm (which is very poor) with bone dust. He has offered $5.00 a ton for all the bones that can be collected and wants 30 or more

---

[2]John. A. Hostetler, Amish Society (Baltimore: The Johns Hopkins University Press, 1980), 119.

tons. This is the first attempt in the neighborhood to use bone manure.

June 10, 1846: David Mast whom I mentioned last winter as having erected a bone mill, strewed or sowed a quantity of bone dust upon poor forest land on which he sowed oats. A small patch of land was left unstrewn and the difference is remarkable. On the land on which the bone dust was applied the oats is (*sic*) equal to any in the good valley land, while on the other it is merely "forest oats."[3]

The Amish have continued to stay close to the land as the decades and centuries have added up. The farms are usually passed from one generation to another and stay in one family forever. The youngest son is the most likely to inherit the farm if he is married. An unmarried son is not a good prospect because it is considered essential to have a wife and a family to make a success of farming. The Amish children are responsible for some chores from early childhood, but are given full adult responsibilities by the time they finish their formal schooling at age fourteen. For the sons who will not have the farm handed down to them, there is the option of renting land to farm and, eventually, buying the property. These young men will probably be marrying and receive a substantial dower from their own parents and their wife's, also. The family is always there to help the young adults establish their independence and become successful at their chosen life's work. The Amish do not accumulate vast amounts of farmland, however, because they need only enough to subsist and care for their own family. The concept of amassing great wealth is contrary to their religious beliefs. Their only goal is to have enough money saved to help their children buy land and establish their own households and to support the members of the community who are needy and

---

[3] Grant M. Stoltzfus, "History of the First Amish Mennonite Communities in America," Mennonite Quarterly Review. 28 (October 1954): 256; in Steven M Nolt, A History of the Amish, (Intercourse, Pennsylvania: Good Books, 1992), 96.

not rely on aid from outsiders. Their philosophy of hard work and self-sufficiency was expressed by one of their early sixteenth century Anabaptist leaders, Menno Simmons, "Rent a farm, milk cows, learn a trade if possible, do manual labor, as did Paul, and all that which you then fall short of will doubtlessly be given and provided you by pious brethren."[4] This statement, written nearly 300 years ago, aptly puts into perspective the Amish farmer's conviction today.

Most Amish farms are dairy farms with a wide variety of crops grown to support the dairy herd. The majority do not grow crops exclusively as a source of income. Crop rotation is used and follows basically the same plan as was developed more than 200 hundred years ago by their Swiss and German forefathers. They raise cows, horses, pigs, fowl and sheep. They have a large and varied vegetable garden for the family's use and, often, an orchard as well as berry bushes as sources of fruit. They make butter and cheese and use the eggs and meat of the fowl, pigs, sheep and, sometimes, beef cattle. The Amish have always relied on the Old Farmer's Almanac and other publications with weather forecasts and planting tables to help them make the most of Mother Nature's gifts. They believe that they can best maintain their self-sufficiency and continue to conform to the tenets of their religion by being general farmers on reasonably small amounts of land. The Typical Amish farm is usually between 80 and 100 acres. To own a lager farm would lead to pridefulness and an overabundance of crops and income, both of which are counter to the Amish way of life. Although they have been criticized for not increasing production in times of need, they have remained staunch. Following World War II they were urged by the U. S. government to produce "more grain for starving peoples of the world," the bishops issued a firm response, stating that they were growing more food with horsepower than their neighbors were with tractors. Every member

---

[4]Menno Simmons, The Complete Writings of Menno Simmons, (Scottdale, Pennsylvania: Herald Press, 1956), 451, in John A. Hostetler, Amish Society, (Baltimore: The Johns Hopkins University Press, 1980), 118.

of the Amish community had already plowed every square inch of his farm by April while their neighbors with tractors were just starting to plow. "Our hearts go out to hungry people wherever they are, and plowing and planting take place right under the fences."[5]

The Amish are using many of the same farming methods that they brought with them from their homelands in Europe. They have taught their non-Amish friends some of their techniques and were at the forefront of agriculture during the eighteenth and nineteenth centuries. Then, the industrial revolution came along and by the early decades of the twentieth century, the Amish were faced with a great and wonderful variety of new and more efficient farm equipment. But, these terrific inventions caused some upheaval among the various factions within the Amish communities. The conflict was between the faster mechanized way of farming and the ideology of the Old Order Amish that working the land is a Godly way of life and providing for one's family is enough. But, change does have a way of creeping into the Amish lives. Some of it came without much notice and other changes caused considerable disruption in the quiet lives they led. As early as the late 1880's there were large steam engines in use on Amish farms for threshing and smaller gasoline engines were allowed to help saw wood, grind feed and power washing machines. These continued to be in use into the twentieth century, but horse and mule power was the only way any of the farmers had to plow, cultivate and harvest their crops.[6] The tractor did not make its way onto American farms until after World War I, becoming a common sight during the 1920's. They were unwieldy and awkward, difficult to steer in the fields and really, just a lot of trouble. The Amish soundly rejected the ungainly machine when they first became common on the American scene. They felt the large wheels would destroy the soil by packing it down and they were too worldly to be on an

---

[5]Hostetler, 125.
[6]Donald B. Kraybill, The Puzzles of Amish Life, (Intercourse, Pennsylvania: Good Books, 1990), 52.

Amish farm. They knew that their horses and mules could get onto the fields much earlier in the spring and their plowing was always done before their "English" neighbors' was. However, some adventurous amish farmers began to experiment with the monstrosities and by the 1920's about a dozen Amish farms in Pennsylvania had the "sod packers" (a slang term used by the amish to describe the large, heavy steel-wheeled early tractors) in use. Oral tradition has it that Moses King took his newly purchased tractor out in the field and started to do the harrowing. The dealer he had bought the tractor had not explained to King how to stop the machine, so he just drove in circles until it ran out of gas and quit! Some Amish farmers had accidents with the tractors, overturning them due to a lack of experience in driving and maneuvering the equipment. Another story of the trouble caused by the tractor involved Ike Zook, who, around 1920, was using his tractor to do his plowing. His neighbor was Deacon Jonas Beiler, brother of the reproachful bishop Ben Beiler, who thought the tractor was the most ridiculous thing to use in the fields and he was annoyed by the noise from the engine. So, deacon Beiler tied his horses to a post and walked over to where Zook was working and told him, "Now you have to get rid of this stupid thing. I'm offended by it." Zook was reprimanded by his church leaders and asked to make a confession in front of the congregation about the use of the tractor. He refused. He liked his tractor so he left his church and joined the more liberal Peachey Church, which had originated through a group of disgruntled Old Order Amish farmers who saw nothing wrong with the use of tractors and allowed them to be freely used by its members.

Just about this same time two Amish ministers from Pennsylvania were visiting the Midwest and found that, even on large farms, the tractor was not in use. They returned to Lancaster County and reported what they had learned. The church leaders concluded that if the large farms in the Midwest could get along without the tractor, then so could the smaller farms of their district.[7]

The process of change among the Amish is one of negotiation and careful consideration of the future impact of the change. The use of tractors, automobiles, electricity or telephones is not considered to be sinful, as such. The concern is what the use of these things could lead to. The tractor controversy is an excellent example of the way in which the decisions are made. The Old Order bishops were keenly aware that the Peachey church, which allowed tractors, also permitted electricity and telephones and that was entirely too worldly. The use of these conveniences might very well lead to more and more dependence on the mechanized world and more and more interaction with the "English," who all had the most modern amenities. Also to be considered was the impracticality of the tractor. It was too heavy to go on the fields in early spring and was so awkward that it was difficult to turn and manipulate. It was also much cheaper to feed a horse than to buy one of the expensive machines. And then, the bishops had already allowed a number of the new farm implements to be used by their members. These included mechanical manure spreaders, hay loaders, tobacco planters and silos. Bishop Ben Beiler also was afraid the tractor was too much like a car, which had already been banned. They both were self-propelled, autonomous and independently mobile. It was possible that the use of the tractor could lead to the use of the automobile. In 1923 the tractor was banned from the fields.[8] The decision was also made to permit the tractors to be used at the barn as a stationary power source for filling the silo, threshing the grain or any other job requiring power for a belt-driven piece of equipment. Further, the tractors must have steel wheels and must only be driven to the site of the job to be done and must never be used as a means of transportation. Horses are still used to pull any powered machinery in the fields. It seemed as though the question of the tractor was settled once, and for all.

---

[7]Donald B. Kraybill, The Riddle of Amish Culture, (Baltimore: The Johns Hopkins University Press, 1989), 172.
[8]Kraybill, The Riddle of the Amish Culture, 173.

However, this was not the case. In the 1940's and 1950's, many smaller, cheaper and more easily handled tractors were on the market. The "English" farmers were virtually all using tractor power on their farms and the Amish were, again, tempted. Some of them defied the earlier ruling of the church leaders and bought tractors to use in the fields. The new hay balers, hay crushers, grain combines and corn harvesters were heavy and difficult for the horses to pull. But, the bishops held fast. Having seen what had happened in other Amish communities when tractors were allowed, one of them said, "Before you know it, they put rubber tires on the tractors and the next thing they are driving them to town for groceries. As the new generation grows up they can't understand the difference between using a tractor for a business trip to town and a car, and so they get a car." They, again, banned the tractor from the fields of Lancaster County in the early 1940's.[9]

But the newly developed farm equipment just kept coming on the market and the Amish farmers were creative enough to invent a way to satisfy the bishops' ruling on tractors and still have the power of the tractor motor at their disposal. They invented the "Amish tractor," a gasoline engine mounted on a four-wheeled cart that could be hooked up to a variety of pieces of farm equipment. The power unit was pulled by the teams of horses to satisfy the orders of the church leaders concerning farm machinery, "If you can pull it with horses, you can have it."[10] One of the concerns of the Amish farmer is where to find horse-drawn equipment. In the fast-paced world of today's modern agribusinesses, there is no room for the manufacture of antiquated farm machinery. They have come up with some adaptations, such as a "fore cart" which goes between the horse and the machinery designed to be tractor-drawn. This does make it possible for them to use some of the modern equipment and remain within the *Ordnung* of the church.

---

[9]Kraybill, The Puzzles of Amish Life, 56.
[10]Kraybill, The Riddle of Amish Culture, 174.

Other concessions were made to the farmers by the bishops. These included permitting the use of stationary diesel engines for power sources for things like drills and saws and battery power for some light sources and various other necessities of farm life. But as progress in farming continued, so did the dissention among the Amish and their church leaders. As the productivity rose, so did the size of the Amish farmers' herds. They were able to grow enough feed crops to support two or three times the number of cows they had in the years before the new equipment and fertilizers and hybrid seeds came on the market. As the dairy herds grew to 24-36 or more, the need for increased storage space for hay and grain was obvious. The hay baler provided part of a solution because it could put the hay into tight, compact bundles and it would take up far less space than putting the loose hay into the mows at harvest. Again, the bishops and ministers were faced with a dilemma concerning their farm-based community. The baler was really a practical solution to the storage problem, but it was designed to be pulled by the forbidden tractor. They were modified by Amish farmers to be used with the "Amish tractor" and, so, conformed to the rules. The church leaders had little choice but to allow the baler, which did solve a major storage problem and save money for the farmers, to be used, but only if it had steel wheels. The Amish bishops have continued to meet the farm equipment challenge head on and held regular meetings to discuss their concerns.

By the 1960's, there were some pieces of self-propelled machinery in use on Amish farms. The introduction of the modern corn harvester to replace the corn binder which had cut the corn stalks and bound the stalks into tidy bundles to be loaded on the wagons and taken to the barn, would cut up the green corn and shoot it up into a wagon pulled behind through a long spout-like device. The ground up corn was then blown into the silo. Another of the problems was the grain binder which was used in the field to cut and separate the grain in one operation. This was a major labor-saving device as the old method was to cut the grain with a machine that tied it up into bundles that then had to be stood up to form neat shocks or stacks to dry. The dried shocks were then threshed in the field and the straw and grain hauled to the barn. Both of these inventions lightened the farmers' work load and added to the bishops' burden. Finally, the church leaders outlawed the two machines. They were concerned that they had let the baler slip through some years before and they did not want more self-propelled machinery to slip through. The corn harvester saved time and labor but did not improve upon the storage method. The Amish farmers did not plant enough wheat to warrant the combine's use, they reasoned, and they felt they had to exercise control over the rapid expansion of the Amish farms. For these reasons they voted to ban the use of the corn harvester and the combine. The bishops have allowed gasoline engines to be mounted on some equipment. The cornbinder was adapted by an Amish mechanic to be horse-drawn, but to have a gasoline engine mounted on it. They had used ground-driven corn binders before this, but the farmer-inventor explained, "We put engines on the corn binders because there weren't enough ground-driven binders around anymore and to keep from the harvesters and combines." The gasoline engine driven corn binder was a compromise and had on its side a number of factors favorable to its use:

It kept modern harvesters off Amish fields

It retained the symbolic horse

It provided plenty of work for farmhands

It permitted silage harvesting to continue in the basic tradition of the past

It eliminated the difficulty of buying scarce ground-driven binders

It created new jobs for Amish mechanics who manufactured replacement parts

It provided extra power to cut the larger varieties of hybrid corn

It enabled dairy farmers to remain financially

competitive
     It opened the way for bishops to escape from
their political quandary.[11]

     The bishops kept close tabs on the farmers after the major
issues of the mechanized forage harvesters, combines and gasoline powered corn binders were resolved. They were aware that
they still had to be diligent in their quest to keep their farmers
within the boundaries of the *Ordnung* and, yet, give them the
leeway needed to be able to make a living in the modern world
and compete with the "English" farmers. They met often
throughout the 1960's to make decisions relating to the new and
improved farm machinery that was continuously being put on
the market. During these years they decided that there were six
worldly items that had been slipping onto Amish farms they
wanted to ban and have "put away" before they got out of hand.
The items were: combines, forage harvesters, barn cleaners,
power units (Amish tractors), electric generators and deep
freezers.[12] The task of ridding Old Order Amish farms and homes
of the six items was more than the bishops bargained for. They
met solid resistance as they continued to debate the issue with
their church members and attempt to enforce the ruling. There
was such a disagreement among the Amish and the bishops that
in 1966, a group of liberal Amish broke away and formed the New
Order Amish church. They continued to use the modern farm
machinery and have electricity in their homes.[13] Since that time,
some modifications have occurred in the Old Order Amish rules
on machinery, but the ban on tractors in the fields has held fast.
     The Amish continue to toil for long hours in the fields and in
the barn, using relatively primitive machinery and equipment.
What follows is a schedule of a typical Lancaster County, Pennsylvania Amish farmer over the period of one year. It is offered
to help the reader gain an appreciation for the kind of life the

---

[11]Ibid., 180.
[12]Ibid., 183.
[13]Ibid., 179.

Amish farm family lives. The schedule includes caring for a tobacco crop, which is typical only in that location and is falling out of favor as a cash crop today. All other chores and activities are typical of an Amish dairy farm:

In **January** the few farmers who have not finished stripping their tobacco complete this work. If steers are being fed, they receive considerable attention at this time so that they will be ready for market whenever prices seem favorable. January, like December, is a popular month for the slaughtering of meat animals. If the winter is mild, apple trees may be trimmed. Frequent visiting is done during this month.

Harnesses are mended and greased in **February**. If there is little frost in the ground, the farmer begins to plow. During February and March, when the curtain is about to rise on the farming season, farmers who wish to retire or restrict their operations hold farm sales. Items offered for sale are usually confined to farm machinery, stock, harnesses, household items and stored grains and feeds. These sales are not only business occasions but also important social events, providing men, women and children with an excellent opportunity for visiting. School teachers find it expedient to dismiss students when sales take place in their neighborhood. Many sales are attended during March even if there is no need to buy anything.

Manure is hauled during the winter months when the ground is frozen and dry. When the ground is in the right condition, the fields are plowed. Clover or alfalfa seed is sowed in the wheat field. Liming requires the attention of some farmers during **March**. Tobacco beds are sterilized with steam, and some vegetables are sown in the garden.

Potatoes are planted as early in **April** as possible. Tobacco seed is sown in the sterilized tobacco bed. Farmers who raise oats seed the crop during this month. The ground is well prepared for corn planting. The garden receives much attention and is prepared from the barn. Corn is generally planted during the last week in April or early in **May**. Toward the end of May, the young tobacco plants are transplanted into the field. More vegetables are planted in the garden. If the growing season begins early, the cultivation of corn and potatoes is begun in the last part of May.

The transplanting of young tobacco plants continues until some time early in **June**. These plants are transplanted at intervals so that the crop will mature over a period of time and can be harvested properly at the right moment. Corn and potato cultivation begins or continues in June, and the operation is repeated four to six times. Potatoes need to be sprayed at least once a week. In early June alfalfa is ready for the first cutting. A week later, the mixed clover and timothy hay may be ready to cut. This crop is generally cut only once, whereas alfalfa is usually cut three times in the season. As soon as the hay is dry it is baled in the field and stored in the barn. None of it is stacked outside. Barley is generally ready to be harvested by the middle of June. Wheat, if it matures early, is ready to be harvested late in June. The grain is shocked in the field after it is cut so that it will dry thoroughly. After a few days it is threshed in the field or in the barn. The straw, however, is nearly always stored in the barn whether it is baled or unbaled.

In **July**, the cultivation of corn and potatoes continues. The whole tobacco patch is thoroughly hoed early in the month and this work engages the entire family. The threshing of small grains begins early in July and may continue into August. Threshing is accomplished through work exchanges with extended family members or neighbors.

August is often a slack month and family members may travel to see distant relatives. Sometime in August, the tobacco-cutting gets into full swing and the alfalfa is ready to be cut the second time. Some early potatoes are dug in the latter part of the month.

September and **October** are very busy months. In September the silos are filled and the cutting and storing of tobacco is completed, safely ahead of an early frost. During the latter half of the month potatoes are dug and the corn is harvested. Each of these tasks generally requires several days of work. Farmers begin to buy steers for winter feeding. The digging and marketing of potatoes may well last until the middle of October.

The corn harvest may continue until **November**. Generally the corn stalks are shredded in November to be used as feed. In this month some farmers will remove loose stones from the fields. **December** is the month for stripping tobacco and the feeding of steers may receive attention. A good deal of butchering is done. Visiting is frequent and perhaps prolonged. With few exceptions, weddings are reserved for November and December.[14]

---

[14]Walter M. Kollmorgen, <u>Culture of a Contemporary Community: The Old Order Amish of Lancaster County, Pennsylvania</u>, "Rural Life Studies No. 4," (Washington, D.C.: U.S. Department of Agriculture, 1942), 43, in John A. Hostetler, <u>Amish Society</u>, (Baltimore: The Johns Hopkins University Press, 1980), 134-136.

The preceding has, of course, undergone changes as the cash crops of potatoes and tobacco have been altered with the market. Also, the Amish in locations other than Lancaster County will be doing different kinds of activities, depending on the type of farming being pursued.

Although farming is the occupation of the majority of Old Order Amish, there are increasing numbers of Amish making a living in non-farming occupations. This shift of employment from self-sufficient farmer to tradesman or craftsman has been gradual, but inevitable, due to several factors. With the demise of the horse and buggy as the dominant means of transportation for Americans, the Amish found that they were forced to learn to repair and construct their own buggies and the harnesses to go with them. Then, as the tractor gained prominence among "English" farmers and more and more tractor-drawn equipment was produced, the Amish farmers needed machinists and mechanics who could both repair their outmoded horse-drawn machinery and adapt the new equipment to a horse-drawn mode. These trades represent little threat to the Amish way of life, as they support the rural, agriculture lifestyle basic to them. Other trades that are natural extensions of the Amish way of life are carpentry, cabinetmaking, horseshoeing, lumber milling, diesel and gasoline engine repairing, painting and masonry. The Amishmen who engage in these trades do not necessarily have to mingle and interact with the "English" population, as there is usually enough work among their own community to keep them quite busy.

Another reason for the shift to entrepreneurial pursuits and cottage industries is the decline in the amount of farmland available. As their population grows, the Amish are having problems finding enough tillable acreage to support their families in close proximity to their church communities. The result is a dwindling in the number of full time Amish farmers and an increase in the number of men and single young women who are engaged in work outside the home. Married Amish women rarely have jobs away from home. Their most important job is child-rearing and nurturing. Many of the cottage industries involve quilts, crafts and items to answer the demands of an ever-growing tourist market. Many Amish women sell their produce and baked goods from small stands along the roadsides. The small operations that employ just a few people and rely on family members for manpower are often in a little building nearby the family home. These shops supply goods and services for both the Amish community and outsiders. The wives are often the bookkeepers and the children are the employees. There are now many construction and carpentry crews among the Amish that do any number of jobs, for both communities, from repairing slate roofs to building homes. Yet another type of Amish-owned business is the retail trade. From drygoods to furniture and crafts, these are often operated out of Amish homes.

As with every aspect of Amish life, the church leaders have much input and control over what types of businesses are permitted and how large the business is allowed to grow. The Amish do not own businesses that offer products and/or services that they are not permitted to use. For instance, an Amishman would never be found as an autobody repairman or manufacturing worldly jewelry or clothing. The bishops and ministers have reached the conclusion that it is better to have members of their flock go into businesses for themselves than to have them go to the factories to work. There, the control would be considerable weakened. They would be in direct and concentrated contact with outsiders and constantly exposed to the worldly concepts the "English" believe in. Then there are problems with social security taxes (the Amish are, for the most part, exempt) and the health insurance. They believe in taking care of their own and do not ever buy insurance, of any sort. Also, labor union membership is forbidden because the way strikes are carried out is against the passive nature of these people. Additionally, the rigid factory work schedule would make it difficult for those working outside of the community to participate in mutual-aid projects, work frolics, barn raisings and the weddings, funerals and other social events that make up such a large part of the Amish culture. Further, it is believed that the father's influence and presence are needed at home, and regularly scheduled work away from there would have a negative effect on the family unit.

Where there are large settlements of Old Order Amish, there is usually a flourishing tourist industry. This is a two-edged sword for Amish families. On the one hand, they attempt to guard their privacy and maintain their separateness from the rest of society, which becomes increasingly more difficult as thousands of tourists inundate their rural areas and seek them out. In Lancaster County, Pennsylvania the tourism business has thrived and flourished as a result of the tourist promotion activities of the local officials. The Amish did none of the promoting, yet they are the focus of the effort. The commercial ventures in the area have gobbled up precious farmland and the result is a shortage of suitable acreage in the vicinity. To gain an impression of the magnitude of the tourist business there, some statistics are needed. During the 1950's the concept was born and the Amish were touted as a reason to travel to Lancaster County. By 1965, two million tourists were making the trip annually. Just nine years later, the number had increased to three million, and in 1993, an incredible five million people were touring the area, feeding the coffers of local businesses and agencies...and threatening the Amish way of life.[15]

The vast majority of the Amish attractions are run by enterprising business people who are neither Amish nor particularly interested in portraying these unique folks realistically.

But, the Amish are reaping some financial benefits from the influx of humanity who want to observe their quaint, peaceful lifestyle. There are far more roadside produce and baked goods stands along the byways of Lancaster County. There are many more cottage industries which are supported by the sightseers

---

[15]Mindy Brandt and Thomas E. Gallagher, "Tourism and the Old Order Amish," Pennsylvania Folklife, 43 (Winter 1993-4): 72.

who are quite willing to pay well for the high quality handmade furniture, crafts, quilts and other wares sold by the Amish. The proximity of the area to New York, Washington, Baltimore and Philadelphia and the paradox of the Old Order Amish who live a nineteenth century lifestyle makes the heart of Pennsylvania's Amish country an ideal place to establish such a successful tourist attraction. The danger would seem to be in the possibility that such a commercial accomplishment may be the very reason the Amish leave that area and seek more private homes where the farmland is more readily available.

Chapter 6
Amish Social Life

Old Order Amish social life is, like all aspects of their existence, family and church community oriented. The activities that
provide social experiences are frequent and inexpensive. While
the typical modern "English" family might well spend a considerable amount of money on the pursuit of recreation the Amish
seem not to find that necessary. Their culture seems to have a
built-in social life. They find their entertainment within their
families and on a very simple scale. The preaching service on
alternate Sundays is an opportunity to share news and concerns.
The wedding of a young couple is a major social event. The
singings provide diversion for the young people of courting age.
Sister's days are looked forward to, as are quiltings and "bees".
Barn raisings and frolics are work sessions which also serve a
social function. Farmer's markets and auctions are gathering
places for the Amish to chat and catch up on the news of the
community.

Visiting family and friends, the older members of the community and the sick are some of the most frequent leisure-time
activities and are a vital part of Amish life. Family ties are
important and even if the adult children are far-flung and great
distances are involved, the parents and grandparents make a
concerted effort to visit frequently. The children, in turn, also
return to the parents' and grandparents' homes to keep the ties
strong and enable the grandchildren to know their grandparents. The Amish do not observe the recognized national holi-

days like Martin Luther King's Birthday, President's Day, Memorial Day, Independence Day, Labor Day, or Mother's Day or Father's Day. They do, however, celebrate a number of religious holidays. These are Good Friday, Ascension Day, Easter, Pentecost, Thanksgiving, Christmas and New Year's Day. Easter Monday, the Monday after Christmas and Whitmonday are celebrated, providing long weekends for visiting and socializing. It is during these extended periods that the Amish are often away from home, traveling by commercial bus or "taxi" to call on relatives who live afar. An Amish "taxi" is a hired vehicle, often a large van, owned and driven by an "English" person. The Amish pay a fee to be taken to various destinations that are too far to reach by horse and buggy. The group of passengers is referred to as the "load." When the Amish travel to distant locales, they often spend one or more nights so that they are able to visit several families. The news of these visits will usually be reported in any of several newspapers that serve Amish populations in numerous locations throughout the country.

Although Christmas is celebrated by the Old Order Amish, it is obviously a religious observance, celebrating the birth of Christ, rather than a grossly commercialized affair to glorify retailing. There is no Santa Claus and no Christmas tree or decorations festooning the home. Instead, there is a family-oriented day of simple pleasures and reverence. In this poem by Barbara Yoder Hall, who was born into a strict Amish family, a typical Amish Christmas is described:

Amish Christmas...

no trees, no trimmings, no toys, no Santa, but,
no sympathy needed.
Different world...secluded and sheltered.

No electric...so no stereo, TV's, radios, cassette
recorders, electric trains.

Christmas was simply-

the birth of the Christ child,
a day of rest.
I loved resting on Friday, or Tuesday, or Saturday. For no
apparent reason.

Oh but, Christmas WAS different.
Breakfast was better...
No mush, no oatmeal,
Instead,
fried potatoes, sausage, eggs, fresh butter, biscuits.
buttermilk...AND one gift,
unwrapped, beside our plate...a practical school item.
Sometimes a ruler, or Eversharp, or a box of Crayolas.

Christmas really WAS special.
Our only candy of the year...a block of chocolate...a
knife stuck in the middle to chip off pieces all day, and
the next,
if there was any left over.

Oranges, too...juicy run-down-your-arm kind.
Chocolate and oranges all day,
what a delight.

Oh yes, the year of the sled.
"It stood in the smokehouse between the hams and the
sausage for two weeks'", Dad said.
"where did you get the money for it ?" an older and wiser
sibling asked.
"I sold a cow," he said simply.
"Good," I said.
"One less to milk."
"Smaller milk-check," Mom said.

Boys rode first while girls did dishes, naturally.

Ten children and a sled,
Two at a time...plus baby.
Baby squealed. Babies don't know you're
supposed to be quiet
Long cumbersome dresses on a sled, but still
happy.
Brother Ferdinand said to me,"I knew it was in the
smokehouse."
"No, you didn't," I told him. "YOU would have
told me."

Today I went shopping...bumper to bumper traffic...
tired clerks, rude people rushing.
I said to myself, but ONLY to myself,
"I'm going back to the year of the sled."[1]

In the home the recreational activities are group oriented.
Many board games are played indoors, as are several clapping
games. One of these, played by adolescent girls at informal
family gatherings, is called "botching." There are variations in
how the game is played, but one common way is for two people
to be seated, facing each other. They clap their palms together
alternately, and alternately clap each other's lap until there is a
very loud clap. Speed is the object and foot-tapping helps with
the rhythm. Often contests take place to see who can go the
fastest. Sometimes the game is played to the tune of "My Darling
Nellie Gray" or "Pop Goes the Weasel."[2] Reading is also popular
as an indoor activity and Amish homes usually always have
ample reading material on hand. Besides the school texts the
scholars might be reading, the other family members read The

---

[1]Barbara Yoder Hall, "Christmas," Broadside, 1982, in John A. Hostetler, Editor, Amish Roots;
A Treasury of History, Wisdom and Lore, (Baltimore: The Johns Hopkins University Press, 1989),
211-212.
[2]John A. Hostetler, Amish Society, (Baltimore: The Johns Hopkins University Press, 1980), 166.

<u>Martyrs Mirror</u>, which tells of the terrible torture and persecution endured by their ancestors, a monthly magazine, *Die Botschaft* ("The Message"), "Reader's Digest," or novels with Christian themes and morals. "The Diary," a weekly newspaper published in Gordonville, Pennsylvania, was begun "by a group of Amish brethren in Lancaster County, Pennsylvania, dedicated to the preservation of fundamental movements of our church in America as well as Old Order religious literature and its virtues," proclaims the masthead. The paper is produced by Pequea Publishers, operated by the Joseph F. Beiler family. In addition, the current news of the Amish community, it concentrates on the genealogies of Amish families and early titles and deeds to property. It used as source material old documents and letters from the early settlements in that area. A committee of bishops and other church officials closely monitors the content of "The Diary." [3]

"The Budget," a weekly newspaper published in Sugarcreek, Ohio, in the heart of the largest Old Order Amish settlement in the world, is an important addition to the Amish home. According to its masthead, it is "A Weekly Newspaper Serving the Sugarcreek Area and Amish-Mennonite Communities Throughout the Americas." With a worldwide circulation, "The Budget" is an important means of exchanging news and information among the Amish and Mennonite communities throughout the globe. Each of "The Budget's" several hundred correspondents sends a weekly "letter" to the paper and they are all published in the 105-year-old newspaper which ranges from 24-30 pages each week. The information shared by the writers includes where church was held and where it will be next time, visitations, sickness and accidents in the community, births and deaths, the weather and how the farm work is progressing. The paper also carries notices of the livestock sales and benefit auctions scheduled in the area, as well as commercial advertising for products and services needed by the Amish readers.

---

[3]Ibid., 368.

Several representative "letters" from Amish reporters for "The Budget," in the unedited form they are received, follow:

"The Budget"

EDGEWOOD, IOWA

July 13 -- It's warm again after a cool spell, when we got a lot of rain. Since my last writing we had around 8 to 10". Our spring was dry. So far summer is very wet and hard to get hay dry. Corn is coming in tassels with a good length. We are looking for the peaches next Mon.

Sun. Church was at Dannie U. and to be at Phineas. Strangers were Amos and 4 children from Beetown, Wis. and Laura H. from Medford, Wis. She is helping out at her bro. Phineas'. Last week a few days Phineas and 2 children and Ada U. were to Medford and brought Laura along back. The young folks, Willie E., Ura E. and the strangers took supper and singing at Dannie U.G.'s.

Marvin J. and Levi N. of Buch. Co. were here a few days helping Daniel N.M. take down a silo at his neighbor's and put it up again at Daniel's.

Tues. John D. got his cast removed. He had a bad broken ankle. The bones are healed pretty good but the ligaments haven't healed so good. He has to go to Guttenburg every few days to get it exercised. Mattie.

QUINCY MICHIGAN

July 15-- We are still having hot and humid weather during the day.

South church was at John (Esther) last Sun. with several families from North church attending.

Bud and Reuben attended the wedding at Linesville at Dan's two weeks ago.

Two weeks ago Jonas, Mike and Vic went to So Whitley leaving sat. p.m. and spent the night there. The next day they took Joe and Joe along to the Ft. Wayne Zoo.

Steve are having frolic (this week) Thur., Fri. and Sat. to frame in their house.

Wilma (Mart) had one of the twins (3 years old) to a chiropractor yesterday as she was complaining of her one leg hurting. Just moving her leg a little caused so much pain that he didn't want to even try and treat her, so sent them on to the bone specialist. She couldn't get an appointment anywhere so stopped at Prompt Care. They took x-rays and said they should be very careful how she moves around until they can get her in at a bone specialist, as the ball is almost out of the hip socket. They think it happened when she fell out of the swing last week.

Chris are also having frolic this week to add on some rooms to the upstairs. Mrs. LaVern

LINWOOD, ONT., CANADA

July 11--After laying most of a week or longer and coming through 3 or more inches of rain near midweek, there was a lot of first crop hay put away on Friday and Saturday. Dan K. had a "father pig" killed by lightning and sever sows injured. This happened inside their barn.

We were to church yesterday in North dist. at James with Freundshaft and friends from other parts, they had a good crowd. Next Sunday church in our part (east) to be at Ezra.

Born to Vernon and Pauline on July 5, a son, Titus Vernon. grandparents are Dan K. and Norman. The baby's lungs were not yet fully developed, so he is still in the hospital.

Eighty-five years ago today on July 11, 1909, David had their first son. They named him Andrew after Davids' father and grandfather. David's grandfather Andrew (great-grandfather to baby Andrew) was one of the 4 brothers who came to Canada from Switzerland in the 1820's to 1840's. Andrew, who has his 85th birthday today, is my father-in-law, and in good health for his age. He is a great-grandfather, so that makes it 7 generations since they came to this part of Ontario. Amongst them who are Old Order Amish there's been very little migration, and nearly all of them still refer to this area as "home". The roots go deep. Elmer

UTICA, MINNESOTA

July 12-- We are having occasional showers. Corn is tasseling out and oats is being cut. Second crop hay would be ready to start cutting. Black raspberries are plentiful in the woods. We have picked and canned 23 quart and made 23 pt. of jam. Cukes and green beans are on the menu.

Our church services were held at Edwin with Pre. Roy and Pre. Jake attending from Cashton, Wis. They came on Sat. afternoon an left for home again Mon. afternoon. There were services held in their honor on Mon. forenoon at Eli E.

Our daus. Polly and Mrs. Menno Mary and dau. Martha met with quite a scary experience and accident last night, Polly had gone over to help Mary dress chickens in the afternoon and help do the chores, then all came over and help shock oats. Menno did some milking and came earlier and the women were going to finish choring and come, too.

It was getting later than we thought it should be and just as we were talking about it a car drove in with them. Their horse started running down the hill and picked up speed. They both pulled on the lines, but he went for the other side of the road. They went down a 50 foot embankment going end over end a coup of times, then said it was just crashes and bangs and stones flying, as this wall was limestone.

Mary flew out before they stopped but Polly stayed in till they stopped. Polly thinks the battery hit her on the head. She then went for help, as there were neighbors close by. They got a car to bring them home and took the horse to the nearest police and called the vet. He was soon out to sew where he was cut, as he was bleeding quite fast. Menno and I took Mary and Polly in and had them x-rayed. Polly had a real sore right shoulder and Mary a sore left shoulder. Doctor said they both have very bad bone bruises or injuries and are wearing slings. Mary has whiplash, too. He said that comes from torn ligaments on the side of her neck. Little Martha just had a small cut on her leg.

To all you friends out there of Lela of Canistota, South Dakota, she passed away on June 25th at 11:45 p.m.. She took sick about 2 weeks before and just got weaker and weaker till she passed on. She did many kind deeds in her life.

Allen son Joni and dau. Katie of Clark, Mo. spent some time here with homefolks, bros. and sisters. They spent Tue. in Blair, Wis. with a sister and family. On Wed. they with Menno Sr. and Menno Jrs. spent the day with their sister Martha and family in Cashton, Wisconsin.

We were at Atlee last Fri. night, as Sam and Miriam (Budget scirbe) of Wolcottville, Ind. were there for overnight. They were on their way to Canistota, S.D. Bill and Lovina spent the night with their dad Joe and bro. Abe They left again on Sat. morn. Orva and Enos were also along but spent the night at a motel room. Mrs. Noah [4]

In New Wilmington, Pennsylvania, "The Globe" is a smaller version of "The Budget" which has a full page of local Amish news, written by its team of reporters. Situated in the midst of a large western Pennsylvania Amish community, this weekly has reported the events of the Amish community from its founding 116 years ago. Out of respect for the Amish writers, the letters are printed exactly as they are received. Herewith, a sample of "The Globe's" weekly information from the Amish community it serves.

"The Globe"

FORT PLAIN, NY - July 12 A nice sunny morning is a little cooler after our week of humid days with scattered thundershowers.

Word was received Thurs night of the funeral of Chris of Lawrence, Simon, John and Davey and wife's left Fri morn for the funeral on Sat Returned yesterday Mon. Sam D left Sat for Romulus to accompany his mother here after her about 2 weeks stay also came home last nigh (Dan) Saloma will now stay here for awhile. Also here over Sun from Lawrence were Steve's and Enos and (Enos) Dave's and Steve and there wifes' left for home yesterday. Mon Church was at John J the once from Lawrence Plus Dave's and Dan Rudy J, Jake R and Emanuel R and the

[4]The Budget (Sugarcreek, Ohio), 20 July 1994.

young folks were there for supper.

Our Son Jonathan is still limping around after his fall about 2 weeks ago when he hurt a ligment in his leg when he slipped on a wet spot in the shop.

We got our sweet Cherry yesterday are a little expensive.

Andy S and wife also wanted to return from Lawrence this week after a weeks stay also intended her Bro wedding

John and wife Sam and wife dau Fannie Janathan from Addison gave us a surprise enroute to Newport over Sun. they all had dinner at Andy D calls at Rudy Dave and Dan Mommy and Roman, spent over Supper at Jake H John were at Dan while rest were at our place.

Mrs. Menno

NEW WILMINGTON - July 14

Had a nice shower of rain today. Wheat is being cut and put on shocks. Have had some very warm days.

On Thur. July 7 Chris age 25 yrs passed away funeral was on Sat. a very large funeral. Leves his wife Susie, 3 daus, and one son. His mother and Father, Ben and Emma also 1 bro. and 4 sisters, funeral was on Sat.

On Wed. July 13 Andy J. age 75 yr. passed away. Having had a couple of heat attacks about 5 wks ago. He leaves his wife Leah C. 2 sons Mose B. married to Lizzie Ann. John M. Byler married to Nancy A. Byler, 3 daus. Lydia married to Jos S. Katie married to Eli L. and Sally married to John Also one sister Mrs Emma. Both familes have our sympathy. Funeral on Fri.

Jacob M. and 4 children and Noah J. spend Friday night at the writers and Emma E. and attend the funeral on Sat. of Chris. And returned to their home Sat. eve. to Ky.

Mrs Fannie D. seems to be about the same. Mrs Katie C. also has not been feeling so good.

Mrs Sarah E. of Friendship N.Y. is visiting her friends and relatives in this area.

Dan J. and Levi D. and children had Sun. dinner at Rudy G.

Those at Emanuel J. on Sunday were Dan M., Dan J. and

Elmer R. and children Emma E. Mrs Elmer R.

FREDONIA-STONEBORO,   PA

July 13

Wasn't quite as warm this week. Cools off at night. Had under 60° 2 mornings. We had a severe thunder storm Wed. night with some people having as much as 2 inches of rain. Here we had 9/10.

Middle district church was at Crist C. Sun. Visitors were Eddie from Lewisville, Ohio, Ervin a. Mose C. and Monroe from Atlantic. Toby A. John C. and Andy from North district.

Mrs. Levi L. had a quilting last Wed. to do the quilt for our school Auction. Our girls and Johns girls were there last evening and got it finished.

Wed. evening Albert B., Mrs. Levi M., Joe B., Mrs. Roman, Martha and Andy were in Spartansburg to visit Andy B.

John M. from Conewango Valley N.Y were here in this area last Wed. and Thur. They visited at Wm. Albert., Andy Rabers, Albert Z. than to here for supper and over night. We took them on a call to Mose and Levi M. Wed. evening.

Thur. we took them visiting at Dan J., Ervin than to David for dinner. In the PM. there were special church services for them at Crist C.

They than planned to be at Neal for supper than get the bus in Mercer to head home. We sure enjoyed their visit.

Thur. evening David, Rudy, Ervin C., Mrs. Katie, John A., and Andy went to visit Abe E. in Sugar Grove who is ill with cancer.

Rudy, Andys and Johns came home that night, but the others stayed and I haven't heard since.

Only minutes after Andys left for Sugar Grove their David age 14 sawed his big toe with the chain saw. The children came down here and wanted us to come up. The other neighbors also came and they called Dr. to come out and take a look. He put in 21 stitches to close the wound.

Marvin from Atlantic drove down to John A. Fri. evening and were there overnight. Marvin went along to the frolic that eve to put dry wall on Emma new house there at Albert A.

Amanda came here than Sat. noon then Marvin came in eve after helping all day on the house. Sun. Albert B., Martha & Emma, Johns, Alberts and us and our families went over to the graveyard, also Marvin.

Marvins, Dad and girls were than here for dinner of ice cream and pizza. Marvins left for home in the eve. Mrs. Eli A. [5]

A basic principle of the Amish religion is the concept of mutual aid or a responsibility for others in the community. Simply put, mutual aid means that whenever a tragedy or crisis befalls a family or a member of the community, the rest of the community comes to that family's or individual's assistance. It also means that the Amish do not ever buy insurance, of any type. They have a rather informal way of managing without it which is called the Amish Aid Society, founded in 1870. The Amish Aid Society is fundamentally a community insurance program. Each family is assessed an amount based on $1.00 per $1,000.00 of property valuation. The money is collected by the church district's director and kept in the fund until some disaster necessitates drawing from the central treasury. When the money has been depleted, another assessment is made. There is no regular collection period, because use of the fund varies according to how many times a disaster occurs, but assessments are usually annual.[6]

The concept of mutual aid fosters a feeling of confidence among the Amish and reduces the stress associated with the fear of being wiped out by a major disaster. The sense of security that results allows for a much more tranquil and serene lifestyle and is a great morale-builder within the Amish community.

The most conspicuous manifestation of mutual aid is a barn raising. If an Amish barn is razed by a tornado or destroyed by

---

[5] The Globe (New Wilmington, Pennsylvania), various dates, June, July, 1994.
[6] Donald B Kraybill, The Riddle of Amish Culture, (Baltimore: The Johns Hopkins University Press, 1989), 86.

fire, the entire community comes to rebuild the structure, often in a single day. Very early in the morning, before the sun is up, the buggies begin to arrive at the site of the disaster. Entire families take part in the day's labor, which is offered free of charge. The women and some of the children will be preparing the food for the midday feast and for supper while the men and other children will set about the task of rebuilding the barn. Before the day of the barn raising, the debris has been cleared away to make the builders' task easier. The lumber and supplies have been bought from the Amish Aid Society funds and are on the scene. Very often a portable sawmill is set up near the site of the new barn several days in advance and the timber has been cut. As soon as daybreaks the men begin the building process. As many as several hundred of them will put the floor in place, and erect the supporting timbers, put the siding on and, finally, put the roof in place. Looking ever so much like ants on an anthill, these men seem to have an innate sense of what has to be done and exactly how and when to do it. In reality, there is a sort of supervisor who orchestrates the whole project, but he is inconspicuous about his duties. What a masterpiece of organization! At noon the men form long lines to reach the benches where basins are ready for hand-washing. Then they join another long line, where women serve the main meal, a picnic, which is the result of their efforts all morning. The menu varies, depending on the season and the availability of fresh fruits and vegetables, but there will always be two or more kinds of meat and gravy, loaves and loaves of fresh-baked bread with jams and jellies to go on it, potatoes, several salads, several cooked and fresh vegetables, and baked goods, including pie after pie, after pie, to round out the meal. Although the day is one of intense toil and exertion, there is always an opportunity for conversation, fun, laughter and practical joking. One of the most common pranks is to nail someone's hat to a rafter high up in the roof beams.[7] The work on the barn continues all afternoon as the

---

[7]Mel Horst, <u>Among the Amish</u>, (Lebanon, Pennsylvania: Applied Arts Publishers, 1992), 22.

women and younger children clear away the mess from the meal. All the while, they catch up on the happenings in the area and news of their friends. As the day closes, the men put the tools away and stack the leftover lumber. If they have farm chores, like milking cows, they leave to go home and do that. If they do not have chores to do at home, they may stay for another, lighter meal before going home. The barn is under roof and all that must be done is the inside finish work.

To do the rest of the work on the barn, a frolic may be held. A frolic is a "work party" or get together. Usually not as well attended as a barn raising, a frolic is for the purpose of accomplishing less monumental tasks. If a shed needs to be whitewashed, or a house is in need of paint, or a neighbor has wood to be cut, or if a fence is in need of repair or there is butchering to be done or any number of jobs need to be done, a frolic is called and the men pitch in to do whatever needs to be done. The women may have a frolic to clean the home of an elderly relative, to put up fruits and vegetables, or to make food for a wedding or preaching service or to help a disabled neighbor catch up on the mending and sewing. All of these chores and tasks are done freely and willingly. The frolics are announced in the paper, if time permits, but, most often, the information is spread by the word-of-mouth method. Sometimes there is a little advance notice, but in the case of serious illness or death, the work cannot be delayed and the community rallies around those in need without regard for their own needs or plans. The frolics are, like the barn raisings, a necessity and involve much time and hard labor. But, they also provide a unique opportunity for the Amish to do good works while socializing with friends and relatives.

"Bees" are similar to frolics in that they are for the purpose of getting some needed work done, but they can also provide a courting opportunity for the adolescents of the area. A husking bee might be scheduled in the fall to help someone get their corn off the stalks and get the ears husked for winter storage. The young people gather on an evening and set to work husking the rows and rows of corn shocks in the field. (The corn had already been cut and put in shocks to dry.) The boys dismantle the shocks and each asks a girl to help him husk. The work goes quickly as the young people laugh and talk together, each one hoping to find the red ear of corn that is the signal for the boy to kiss his partner. Then, midway through the evening, there is supper and more socializing, although good-natured chatter and conversations take place for the whole event. The young people usually head for the barn for games after they have finished eating supper. The evening ends at about 1 a.m. when the tired, but happy young adults head for home.

Where farmers' markets are still held, they, too, are a common place for the Amish to gather. Both buyers and sellers are able to see friends and relatives and exchange the news with the ones they have not seen for some time. They are usually family affairs, with the buggies full of children and produce to be sold leaving the farm before dawn. The children are given the opportunity to mingle with the "English" and converse with them, practicing their language skills, while enjoying the interaction. The older children learn to make change and to sell their wares. And, of course, the Amish are constantly chatting among themselves, in their German dialect.

Public sales and auctions serve several functions in the Amish community. They are a natural gathering place for both Amish and "English" bargain hunters. They are somewhat of a tourist attraction, because they provide a showcase of the Amish way of life for the curious onlookers. The men gravitate to the rows of stalls where the livestock wait to be sold to look over a feeder calf or a possible replacement for the aging draft horse that makes up one half of a team. Or, perhaps, to the piles of tools and gasoline engines and harness parts waiting to be sold at a benefit sale. The women form small clusters where they talk of the day's gathering, look over the household merchandise and enjoy a day away from the usual chores, while the children run and romp and play and enjoy each other's company and the good things to eat at the food tables. These auctions make up a significant portion of the social life of the Old Order Amish and are a marketplace for buying and selling goods, whether it's livestock from all over the area or the contents of a farm family's house and barn. Benefit auctions are held when there is an immediate need for more funds than are in the Amish Relief Society's coffers, for a hospital bill or for the expenses of a family who have lost a loved one. All through the summer there are auctions to benefit Amish schools in any number of communities. Auctioneers, both Amish and non-Amish, show up, donate their time and spend the day selling donated items that range from old dishes and glassware to coffee cans full of nuts and bolts and boxes of books. Along with tons and tons of contributed household and miscellaneous items, there are always handcrafted things made by the Amish. There might be several birdhouses and bird feeders, oak and hickory rockers, knickknack shelves, home grown produce, homemade baked goods, porch swings, wooden toys and hand-stitched pillow tops, wall-hangings and quilts! The quilts made by Amish women have become the drawing card for many "English" folks who seek out the auctions to search for the handmade treasures.

The quilts also provide a wonderful opportunity for socializing among the women. The tiny quilting needles seem to fly when a group of Amish women sits around a quilt frame and creates a work of art. To appreciate the artistry of the quilt, it is necessary to know something of the origin of the craft. Always frugal, the early Amish women used the leftover fabric scraps from their sewing and pieces of worn-out clothing to make bedcovers for their families. The patterns seem to be random, but often have a subtle color or shape motif running throughout the quilt. Even though there is some time saved because the pieces are of random shapes and there is not a set design to be followed, much time is consumed in the embroidery that is done all along each seam in contrasting thread. Sometimes there is some intricate design embroidered in the middle of one of the larger patches. Although not the most popular among quilt-fanciers, the crazy quilt can be quite lovely.

As the very early Amish farms in Pennsylvania prospered, the women were able to purchase fabric just for quiltmaking and the crazy quilt fell out of favor. One of the first patterns to emerge was the diamond in square or center diamond. It consists of a large square of one solid color, tipped on its side, to form a diamond in the center of the quilt. Large triangles fill the corners, making another square and one or more borders are added to the central pieces. The borders vary in width and may be broken up by the placing of contrasting squares on the corners. The quilt may have as few as two colors or as many as five. The outstanding thing about this pattern is the large expanses of plain areas which show off the beautifully done quilting. These complex patterns formed by stitches that are quite functional, as well as decorative. The quilt is made up of three layers; the top, which has been pieced or appliqued to form a design, the quilt back, which is one solid color and has no design and the lining, which goes between the other two layers. The lining gives the quilt its warmth and also shows off the quilting stitches because of its puffiness. The stitches are really there to hold the three layers together and do provide a creative outlet for the Amish women who make them. Because it is so very difficult to sew quilt patches together which have rounded edges, the patterns are predominately straight-edged geometrics. The stitching formations allow the quilt's designer to incorporate curves and circles into the overall plan.

Most of the Amish quilt patterns are abstract and have no realism, but just a suggestion of the object depicted. The inspiration for most of the patterns comes from the world they live in. The straight lines of fences surrounding a pasture is a possible basis for the Bars and Rail Fence pattern. The fan designs found in many quilts may be reminiscent of buggy wheels and the pinwheel patterns may have their origin in the water-pumping windmills found on many Amish farms. The star is present in a great number of patterns and probably came from the closeness the Amish feel with the heavens and the seasons.

Although some non-Amish quilters have used printed fabric in their piece-work designs, Amish women use only solid fabrics in quilts for their own use. This is obviously because the fabric scraps from their sewing are all solid colors and that is where most of the cloth for the piecing comes from. (With the increase in the non-Amish interest in owning Amish-made quilts, there are now more and more quilts at Amish sales and in their shops with patterned pieces in the design.) One of the interesting aspects of the Amish quilt is the use of color. The Amish are not educated beyond eighth grade and they have no specialized art appreciation or application classes. Their range of colors permitted by the church is somewhat narrow, with a lot of dark tones and black being used. They do not have to be concerned about whether on not their socks match their dress or which shirt to wear with which trousers. In spite of this, the traditional Amish quilts are vibrant and bright. The women who design the patterns seem to have a non-spoiled, natural ability to put pieces together in such a way as to enhance the overall configuration.

The following description of a quilting is from the work of Rachel and Kenneth Pellman, who have authored a number of books on Amish quilts and quilting.

> A quilting is an all-day occasion to do some fun "work"-and visit. It is generally hosted by a woman who has one or more quilts to be quilted. She may choose to make it a "sisters' day'" whereupon she invites all her sisters or she may issue a broader invitation to various friends and neighbors. Quiltings take place throughout the year but are more frequent during the less busy seasons on the farm.

> Usually quilting begins early in the morning after mothers have given their school-age children a proper breakfast and have seen them off for the day. Pre-school children attend quiltings and,

since there is usually a group of them, have as much fun playing as their mothers have quilting. Older children may be asked to keep a supply of threaded needles on hand and help to watch their younger siblings. The quilt, stretched tightly in a quilting frame, provides a wonderful imaginary house for these youngsters.

The first job to be done (if the hostess has not already completed it) is "putting in" the quilt. That involves stretching the back, lining and top of the quilt tautly in the frame. The most common type of frame allows the quilters to work on all four sides of the quilt at the same time. It is a simple structure with four strips of wood held together by c-clamps. The top and bottom ends of the quilt back are pinned or basted to a strip of heavy fabric which has been tacked along the edge of two of the frame's wooden strips. The back is then tightly stretched between these two strips and the remaining two wooden strips are laid along the sides of the quilt back. The pieces of wood are clamped at the corners, thus making the quilt back a tight, flat surface. The frame, now stretched to its proper size, is then laid across the backs of four chairs making it an appropriate height for quilting. Next, the lining is laid on the quilt back and pinned securely on all sides. and finally the top, with all its tracings for quilting designs, is stretched over the back and lining and pinned tightly in place. The bedcover is ready to be quilted.

A typical quilting will involve anywhere from six to twelve women. Seating positions around the quilting frame are good-naturedly negotiated since no one wants to sit next to and be outshone by the best or fastest quilter! And less experienced quilters choose to sit where there are straight lines to quilt since they are more easily managed than curved lines.

The women, sitting around all four sides of the frame, begin quilting at the outer edge and work toward the center as far as they can reach. When all the women along the top and bottom of the frame have quilted to their maximum reach, the quilt is ready to "roll." The clamps at the four corners of the frame are released and the finished sections of the quilt are gently rolled onto the wood until the unquilted surface is brought to the edge. "Rolling" can take place only from the two ends of the frame. Therefore, when the quilters along the side reach their maximum they must either find and squeeze into a new position at the ends, begin another quilt in another frame or find something else to do. Those who choose the latter frequently help the hostess prepare lunch.

The noon meal is compensation for the time and effort supplied by the invited quilters. It is the highlight of the day. The hostess prepares a full-course meal and serves it with pride. Kitchen helpers may be women who were invited to the quilting but would rather not quilt. For them, being in the kitchen is as enjoyable as being around the frame. However,if a woman is assigned to kitchen duty when she would rather quilt, it can be humbling. This sometimes happens to teen-aged girls whose stitches are not yet tiny or neat enough to meet the hostess' quilting standards. It is an honor for young girls to be invited to quilt at a quilting. Quilting resumes again after lunch. Women are free to come and go as they are able. Some stay the whole day. Others come for only a few hours.

A quilting is more than just a work day. It is an occasion to share household tips, garden hints, home remedies, child-rearing information and the latest news about marriages, births and deaths. Such a gathering of women with common interests, backgrounds and goals provides a chance for them to talk at length about their daily lives. A quilting reminds these women of the support they have and gives them a break from the daily routine. For the hard working farm women, such an event can be a refreshing one-day vacation.

Quiltings are not only held in private homes. The Amish, though separate from the larger world, are not unaware of global needs. Amish women readily participate in quiltings held by the Mennonite Central Committee, a world-relief organization that sends food, clothing and personnel all over the world. Amish women also lend their skills to community projects. Many volunteer fire companies hold quiltings several times a year to produce quilts to sell at their benefit auctions. Since the Amish rely on the services of their local fire companies, they support them actively as volunteer firefighters and contribute time and energy to their quiltings and benefit suppers.

When a quilting day is ended and the quilt completed, it stands as a tangible symbol of group effort. It portrays not only the skill of these women, but also the strong supportive love that envelopes this community and keeps it vibrant and alive despite the pressures of the modern world.[8]

---

[8]Rachel and Kenneth Pellman, The World of Amish Quilts, (Intercourse, Pennsylvania: Good Books, 1984), 82-83.

Chapter 7
Going to Church

To the Old Order Amish People, "the church" is not a building, but, rather, a way of life. Although they are deeply religious, the Amish avoid the established accoutrements and outward symbols of religion. There are no buildings with steeples and bells, no altars, no paid clergy, no collection plate, no parsonage or rectory, no choirs and no pews or kneeling rails. Their entire life is a testimonial to their profoundly religious culture. They have as a reason for everything they do, a Scriptural reference which is not subject to drastic change or to questioning. Their very existence is the result of disputes with others who shared similar beliefs during the sixteenth century in Switzerland, but had deviated from the very strict adherence to the Scriptures. They began as Anabaptists, a group of religious zealots who believed that infant baptism was not appropriate because of the magnitude of the decision and the seriousness of the vows taken during the ritual. They were founded when, in defiance of the Zurich government, they held secret Bible reading and prayer services. At one of these sessions, in 1525, a man named George Blaurock asked Conrad Grebel to baptize him and it was done. Thus began the Anabaptist movement and the hope for religious freedom. They continued to conduct services and to baptize the adults in their group, using as the basis for their beliefs the New Testament, especially the teachings of the Sermon on the Mount. In addition they believed in the literal obedience to the teachings of Christ, adult baptism, social separation from the evil world, exclusion of errant members from communion, mutual aid, rejection of violence, the refusal to swear oaths, the autonomy of each congregation and the separation of church and state. They were immediately subject to persecution at the hands of both Protestant and Catholic authorities and were forced to continue to hold their services in secret locations during the wee hours of the night.

To avoid the unspeakable atrocities and torture the government and the Protestant and Catholic leaders inflicted upon these people, they were forced to flee to locations with more sympathetic populations and governments. One of the migrating groups of Anabaptists had broken away from Conrad Grebel, and was being led by Menno Simons. Simons' followers went with him to Holland, where religious freedom already existed. This group became known as Mennonites and they continued to adhere to the basic tenets set forth by Conrad Grebel, while remaining separate from the other Anabaptist factions. The bases for the beliefs and standards of behavior of the Mennonites were set down in 1527 in the Schleitheim Confession of Faith and the later Dortrect Confession of Faith. Both of these documents were very specific in their directives and both endorsed the practice of *Meidung* or "shunning" or avoiding excommunicated members.

One Mennonite bishop, Jakob Ammann, who had studied the Bible and both Confessions of Faith extensively, felt that the followers of Menno Simons were straying too far away from the stringent and literal interpretation of these writings. During 1693, Ammann was so concerned about this liberal movement among the Mennonites that he began to visit all of the congregations in Switzerland and the adjacent Alsace, where Simons' followers had eventually settled. He was unwavering in his insistence that the absolute and literal interpretation of the Bible must be the foundation of their beliefs. As he traveled among the congregations, demanding total obedience to his tenets, he met with some opposition. There were those who believed that a degree of deviation was acceptable and would not jeopardize the church's existence or the souls of the members. Following a series of heated discussions with the ministers and bishops of the congregations, Jakob Ammann and his contingent of advocates broke away from the Mennonites during the 1690's and formed their own church, which became known as the *Ammansch* then, eventually, the Amish.

Down through the centuries there have been subtle changes in the practices of the Amish and, on several occasions in their history, there have been major upheavals which caused irreconcilable differences that resulted in other factions breaking away from the original group. That accounts for some of the dissimilarities among the Amish congregations. But, basically the Old Order Amish conduct their lives and hold to the same beliefs in modern times as they did 300 years ago when they began. Because they had to hold their services in hiding, often barns and private homes were used for worship. As the Amish traveled about Europe searching for religious freedom there was no opportunity to erect church buildings and after they immigrated to Pennsylvania and had total religious freedom, they chose to retain the practice of worshipping in their homes. The preaching services are held every other Sunday in the home of one of the members. The service rotates from one home to another and, eventually, every family in the church district hosts services. A church district or *Gemei* is defined by geographical area and refers to the congregation, or all of the church members in that designated area. The number of families in the *Gemei* is determined by the sizes of the homes and how many people they can hold for services. The average church district has 25 families or 75 adult members, in addition to all of the unbaptized children and young adults who also attend the preaching services.

An Amish community is made up of several congregations or church districts. There is no formal church leadership at the state, provincial, national or international level because, since their earliest history, the Amish churches have retained their autonomy. All of the decisions regarding the congregation in a church district are made by the officials of that group. In the earliest Amish churches there were four officials although just three are customary in today's organizational plan. The three are called Diener (servant). The first is the *Volliger Diener* (minister with full powers) or bishop, who is the spiritual leader of the congregation and is permitted to perform the rituals of baptism, marriage, communion, funerals and ordination. He also takes a turn preaching Sunday sermons in rotation with the preachers. He is also authorized to make pronouncements of excommunication, but only after a congregational vote is taken. He is also the arbiter in any disputes within the group and has the final determination concerning the clothing styles, buggy styles and details of everyday life. The bishop is given the following lifetime charge at the time of ordination:

> (1) So in the name of the Lord and of the church, the complete ministry or bishop's office is entrusted to you (2) that you shall declare the Lord's bitter suffering and death and observe the breaking of bread and wine (3) and if there are people who wish to unite with the church, then you shall teach them the Christian faith and baptize them (4) and, with the council of the church, you shall punish the disobedient and sinners, and when they manifest repentance and conversion, you shall receive them again with the council of the church (5) when there are brethren and sisters in the church who wish to marry you shall unite them according to the godly ordinance (6) and you shall also ordain ministers with full authority [i.e. bishops], whenever it is necessary and requested in the church (7) and when you become old and weak you are to ordain a man after you in your place (8) and may the Lord strengthen you

with his holy and good spirit, through Jesus Christ
Amen.[1]

The second office in the Amish church is that of *Diener zum Buch* (minister of the Bible) or preacher, who is to help the bishop with duties of preaching and teaching. The delivery of long sermons of two and one half hours or more is his primary responsibility. There may be two men in this position in larger congregations. He may also be called the minister and may be asked to fulfill the duties of the bishop if there is a need because of illness or a vacancy in the office. The preachers are charged at ordination as follows:

> So in the name of the Lord and of the
> church the ministry to the Book is committed to
> you that you shall preach [expound the word],
> read, pray with the church, help protect good, and
> help punish and prevent evil.[2]

The *Volliger Armendiener* (minister of the poor) or full deacon is the position that rarely exists in today's Amish church and was really only used extensively by European congregations. In addition to executing all the duties of the deacon, which are listed below, he may also have been called upon to help with baptisms and to preach sermons. He was also in charge of correcting any errors made by the preachers and bishops during their sermons.

The last of the four officers is the *Armendiener* or deacon. This person's main functions are to read scripture and lead prayers during services, to assist with baptisms and communion and to oversee the "alms fund" of the church. This fund is for mutual aid of any needy ones in the congregation. He may be asked by the bishop to make home visitations when there is a question of church rules being violated. He is also the bearer of good or bad news, being the bishop's messenger in cases of excommunications or reinstatement. He meets with prospective marriage partners when a wedding is imminent. The deacon's

---

[1] John Umble, "Amish Ordination Charges," <u>Mennonite Quarterly Review</u>, (October, 1939), 236.
[2] Ibid., 237.

charge at the time of his ordination is:

> So in the name of the Lord, and of the church, the ministry of the poor is committed to you that you shall care for the widows and orphans, receive alms and give them out with the counsel of the church and if there are brethren and sisters who wish to enter the marriage state, then you shall serve them according to the godly order and read the scriptures for the ministers when it is requested and shall serve the water in the baptismal ceremony, if you are requested to do so.[3]

These officials represent the power structure of the Old Order Amish church. They have consultations during the worship services and other times, if necessary. Virtually all decisions regarding the lives of the congregation's members rest with these men, with the bishop as the most powerful of them all. The preachers and deacons are elected by the congregation from among the married males in the group. Although women who are church members have a vote, they are not permitted to hold any offices. The bishop is chosen from among the deacons. The bishop is chosen by "the lot," and will hold the office for life, or until he is unable to perform his duties. The Bible has directed the Amish to choose their leader according to Acts 1: 24-26, concerning the replacement of Judas as one of the disciples after he betrayed Christ. "And they prayed, and said, Thou, Lord, who knowest the hearts of all men, show of these two which one Thou hast chosen, to take the place in this ministry and apostleship from which Judas fell away, that he might go to his own place. And they gave lots for them and the lot fell upon Mathias and he was numbered with the eleven apostles. When there is a need to select a new bishop, this is announced during the service and a two-week period of prayer and serious discussion. The ordination is frequently set to coincide with the semi-annual communion service, the high point of the Amish church rituals. All

---

[3]Ibid., 237.

members of the congregation must agree that an ordination is necessary and the group must be free of dissention and disagreement. On the day of ordination, the men who are eligible are seated on the first bench. The bishop instructs two other men to take an equal number of hymnals as there are candidates to another room. There, a piece of paper called the ordination slip is put into one of the books. One of two Bible verses will be written on this paper. Either Proverbs 16:33, "The lot is cast into the lap; but the whole disposing thereof is of the Lord," or Acts 1:24, "And they prayed and said Thou, Lord, which knowest the hearts of all men, show of these two the one whom Thou hast chosen." The hymnals are placed at the front of the room and each of the candidates rises and goes to select one. The books are handed to the Bishop, one by one, by each candidate and he searches through each one. When he finds it, he announces loudly to the congregation, the name of the man on whom the lot has fallen. The ceremony is accompanied by great suspense and anticipation. When the announcement is made, there will be weeping and murmurs of concern for the man who is now given a great burden to bear. The lot is never refused, as it is the belief of the Amish that the Lord, in His wisdom, knows which man is best suited to carry out the duties of the office. The ordination service follows immediately. All of these church officials are untrained and unpaid. Because it is believed that God is responsible for the choice of all leadership positions, the positions are for life. If a church officer moves to a new community, his ordination stands in the new location as well, giving some congregations multiple bishops and deacons and more preachers than would ordinarily be needed.

It is a major undertaking to host the preaching service and takes nearly a week of labor to see to the preparations. With the help of family and friends, the house is cleaned and scrubbed from top to bottom. The yard is mowed and trimmed and the barn is thoroughly cleaned for the singing to be held that evening for the young people. Sometimes, during warm weather, the barn will be used for the preaching service. The host family must also provide the noon meal for the congregation and an evening meal for relatives who stay on to visit. They are also responsible for providing refreshments for the young people after the singing. Very early on the morning of the preaching service, some of the men and boys arrive with the long, backless benches. The Scriptural basis for this type of seating is found in Amos 6:1, "Woe to them that are at ease in Zion." These oak benches are carried from house to house in a long, enclosed wagon and stored in it when they are not being used for preaching. The walls between first floor rooms are moved aside and the furniture is pushed into the corners to make a large open room where the benches will be set up in rows for the congregation. Sometimes the benches will also be put in the second floor and in the barn if necessary. There will be chairs for visitors and the elderly and infirm.

The service begins at 8:30 a.m. and lasts until about 1:00 p.m. unless there is a communion service, baptism service or an ordination. The men and women sit separately during the service. The older married men are at the front, the others file in behind them and the unmarried young men are in the kitchen, dining room or an upstairs room. The married women sit down after all the men are seated, filling the seats behind the men and spreading out into the other rooms as needed. The preschool boys sit with their father and the preschool girls sit with their fathers. The service opens with a hymn, while the preachers retire to an upstairs room to decide who will deliver sermons that day and to discuss any problems with church discipline. The hymns are sung without musical accompaniment of any kind, are sung in unison and are led by the *Vorsinger*, or song leader. The Biblical directive for singing *a capella* is in Amos 6:5, which warns against those "...that chant to the sound of the viol, and invent to themselves instruments of music like David." This is a man with a knowledge of the tunes and the ability to stay on key. The congregation sings along and the result is not unlike the Gregorian chants of centuries past. All of the hymns are taken from the only hymnal ever used by the Amish, the *Ausbund*, which was printed sometime between 1564 and 1583 (historians are unable to agree on the exact date of printing) and contains 140 songs, in German, written by early Anabaptists during the years of persecution during the Protestant Reformation in Europe. The suffering was so great and the prison conditions so deplorable, that when spirits and morale were sinking, someone would respond with an inspiring, uplifting song of praise and faith of God. The songs of these tortured martyrs are still providing inspiration to the Amish, after more than 400 years. The songs were not written down for a number of years and were simply passed on as part of the oral tradition of the culture. Although they are now in print and used by virtually every Old Order congregation, there are variations in the way they are sung, or chanted. The *Vorsinger* sets the tone and the pace and each of them may present the song a little differently. There are notations, but they are open to a great deal of personal interpretation. Every line takes approximately 30 seconds to complete, making a complete hymn last for quite a long time if it has a number of verses.

Following the first hymn, which varies from Sunday to Sunday, the 'S *Lobg'sang*, or Song of Praise is sung. In every preaching service this is always the second hymn. It is a lengthy one and can last from 20-30 minutes, depending on the Vorsonger. The words of one stanza of the well-known 'S *Lobg'sang* are:

O, God, Father, we praise Thee,
And extol Thy many blessings:
That Thou hast, O Lord, proved
Thyself again so merciful to us;
And hast brought us together, Lord,
To exhort us through Thy word;
Grant us Thy mercy.[4]

The ministers return during this hymn and one of them

---

[4] George Korson, ed., <u>Pennsylvania Songs and Legends</u>, (Philadelphia: The University of Pennsylvania Press, 1949), 144.

"makes the beginning," or delivers the first, or short, sermon, which lasts from 30-60 minutes. Then the congregation kneels in silent prayer and then stands for the deacon's Scripture reading. The main sermon is next and lasts for at least an hour in most Amish churches. As this sermon begins, cookies and crackers are passed down the rows to each of the children, followed closely by a glass of water to wash them down. The service could go on for another two hours and the little ones do get restless. Following that message, a chapter is read from the Bible and testimonies are given by the other ministers or members and any corrections are made. Then, remarks are heard from the minister who preached and a prayer is read. The benediction follows, with the congregation standing, and is followed by announcements (where the next preaching service will be held, whether a membership meeting is needed after the service, news of illness, etc.) and then, the final hymn. Throughout the service, at any time the name of Jesus is spoken, the entire congregation genuflects, as instructed in Philippians 2:10, "That at the name of Jesus, every knee should bend..." At dismissal, the people file out, youngest first, to await the call to the midday meal.

If there are candidates who have completed the required six to eight weeks of instruction and are ready to be baptized, this ritual is included in the preaching service.

The decision to be baptized and become a member of the Old Order Amish church is not to be taken lightly. It is the hope and prayer of every Amish parent that all of their children will make the decision, but there are no guarantees and a parent would never force the young person to join the church against his or her will. The vows are simply stated but represent a lifetime of commitment to a strict and austere way of life. Following the second sermon, in the regular order of things, the applicants for baptism, who are seated in the front row, are reminded that they are about to make a vow with God and are asked to kneel if that is their desire. The deacon has left the room and returned with a tin cup and a bucket of water. The bishop asks the following questions of each applicant:

1. Are you able to confess with the Ethiopian eunuch, that you believe that Jesus Christ is God's son? (Answer: Yes, I believe that Jesus Christ is God's son.)

2. Do you confess that you are uniting with the true church of the Lord? (Yes)

3. Do you renounce the devil and the world with all its wicked ways, and also your own flesh and blood, and commit yourself to serve Jesus Christ alone who died for you on the cross? (Yes)

4. Do you promise to keep the ordinance (*Ordnung*) of the Lord and the church, to faithfully observe and to help administer them, never to depart from them so long as you shall live? (Yes)[5]

The congregation then rises for prayer, while the applicants continue to kneel. With the help of the deacon's wife, who unties the ribbon of the first girl's *Kapp* and removes it. The bishop places his hands on the head of the candidate and says, "Upon your faith, which you have confessed before God and these many witnesses, you are baptized in the name of the Father, the Son and the Holy Spirit, Amen."[6] The deacon pours a cupful of water into the bishop's hands, which are cupped above her head, and the water drips from his hand, down over her head and face. The same procedure is followed for each of the applicants. Following the actual sprinkling of the applicants, they rise and receive the Holy Kiss from the deacon's wife and a welcoming handshake from the bishop. This is a most emotional ceremony, moving many of the congregation to tears, as it is the culmination of all the training and teaching of their lives, up to this point, and it means that the community has been successful in keeping this group of young people within the fold.

Communion and footwashing, held once each spring and

---

[5]John A. Hostetler, <u>Amish Society</u>, (Baltimore: The Johns Hopkins University Press, 1968), 52.
[6]Ibid., 56.

once each fall, are two elements that reaffirm the commitment of members of the Amish church and are part of the fundamental beliefs put forth by Jakob Ammann, 300 years ago. The preparation for this important ritual begins at the service two weeks before the actual communion Sunday. Attendance is required and the service usually takes most of the day. Members are questioned individually as to their preparedness for the communion ritual and confessions, if necessary, are heard. The members are asked to make their peace with the other members and with God at this service. If a member is guilty of an infraction of the rules and does not come forth, he or she is denied the privilege of partaking of communion with the membership. If there are excommunicated members who have confessed, are forgiven, and wish to be taken back into the fold, this can be accomplished on this Sunday of preparation for the most holy ritual in the Old Order Amish culture. It is a time of self-evaluation of the members and a time to draw errant members back onto the straight and narrow. Because of the length of the two days and the serious nature of the rituals, children are often permitted to stay home from both the preparatory service and the communion service. Groups of youngsters gather at several members' homes where a young adult girl who is not yet baptized will look after them. These two services are also closed to outsiders. Fasting and meditation are also part of the preparation which the members must observe the day before the communion service.

The sermons on both days are long and filled with the consequences of sinning and non-obedience to the Scriptures. Although the communion day messages are somewhat more relaxed than the ones delivered at the previous service, they are lengthy and the service goes well into the afternoon. At the end of the second sermon, the bread, which has been baked by the hostess, and the wine, which has been made by the bishop's wife, are brought out and the bishop retells the story of the Last Supper. He breaks the bread and partakes, then drinks of the wine. The bread is then broken and passed to the congregation, as is the cup containing the wine. When all have participated, one of the ministers reads the story of Christ washing the disciples' feet from John 13, while others bring in buckets of water and towels. The members are asked not to be biased and to wash the feet of the person closest to them. While a hymn is being sung, the men wash each other's feet, and when they have finished, the women follow suit. When the service ends, the members leave and present a donation to the church poor fund. This is done so that no one knows the amount contributed by each person, as it is a very private and personal matter.

All of the rules that the Amish live by are collectively called the *Ordnung*, or ordering. This represents hundreds of years of interpretation of the Scriptures by the bishops and ministers of the church. The Amish do not have the Ordnung written down, they simply know the rules because every facet of their lives is controlled by it. The portion of the *Ordnung* that controls attire and outward appearance has been printed in Chapter 3 and will not be repeated. What follows is the remainder of the rules:

"*Ordnung* of a Christian Church"

Since it is the duty of the church, especially in this day and age, to decide what is fitting and proper and also what is not fitting and proper for a Christian to do, (in points that are not clearly stated in the Bible), we have considered it needful to publish this booklet listing some rules and obediences of the Christian Church.

We hereby confess to be one faith with the 18 articles of Faith adopted at Dortrecht, 1632, also with nearly all, if not all, articles in the booklet entitled "*Article und Ordnung der Christlichen Geminde.*"

...No decorations of any kind in buildings inside or out. No fancy yard fences. Linoleum, shelf and wallpaper to be plain and unshowy. Overstuffed furniture or any luxury items forbidden. No doilies or napkins. No large mirrors, (fancy glassware), statues or wall pictures for decorations.

No embroidery work of any kind. Curtains either dark green rollers or black cloth. No boughten (sic) dolls.

No bottle gas or high line electrical appliances. Stoves should be black if bought new.

Weddings should be simple and without decorations. Names not attached to gifts.

No ornaments on buggies or harness.

Tractors to be used only for such things that can hardly be done with horses. Only stationary engines or tractors with steel tires allowed. No airfilled rubber tires.

Farming and related occupations to be encouraged. Working in cities or factories not permissible. Boys and girls working out away from home for worldly people forbidden except in cases of emergencies.

Worldly amusements such as radios, card playing, movies, fairs, etc., to be forbidden. Reading, singing, Bible games, relief work, tithing, etc. are encouraged.

Musical instruments or different voices not permissible. No dirty, silly talking or sex teasing of children.

Usury forbidden in most instances. No government benefit payments or partnership in harmful associations. No insurance. No photographs.

No studying or selling of anything on Sunday. It should be kept according to the principles of the Sabbath.

Church confession is to be made if practical where transgression was made. If not, a written request of forgiveness should be made to said church. All manifest sins to be openly confessed before church before being allowed to commune. 1 Tim. 5:20. A period of time required before taking new members into full fellowship.

Because of a great falling away from sound doctrine, we do not care to fellowship, that is hold communion, with any churches that allow or uphold any unfaithful works of darkness such as worldliness, fashionable attire, bed courtship, habitual smoking or drinking, old wives fables, non-assurance of salvation, anti-missionary zeal or anything contrary to sound doctrine.[7]

Meidung, or shunning, is the ultimate punishment delivered upon an excommunicated church member by the leaders of the congregation and is a most dire response to an infraction of the *Ordnung*, or rules. It was one of the three main tenets espoused by Jakob Ammann when he led his band of followers away from the church of Menno Simons. It is a very effective way of keeping the church free of those who would cast a shadow upon the virtue of the group. The Old Order Amish practice *Meidung* today just as Jakob Ammann preached it three centuries ago. The practice is based on Paul's admonition in 1 Cor. 5:11, "But now I have written to you not to keep company with anyone named a brother, who is sexually immoral, or covetous, or is an idolater, or a reveler, or a drunkard, or an extortioner-not even to eat with such a person." This drastic punishment is delivered only after the offender is asked to change his or her ways. If the person refuses, then he or she would be excommunicated and the *Bann* (avoidance) would be imposed. The hope is that the offender will see the error of his or her ways and make confession before the congregation and ask forgiveness and to be taken back into the fold. During the time that the Bann is in place, there is some social interaction permitted, but it is slight. If business dealings with members are necessary then the excommuni-

---

[7]Amish Church of Pike County, Ohio, "*Ordnung* of a Christian Church," n.d., unpaged.

cated one often has a third party do the actual transaction or places money on a counter or table and from there the member picks it up, thus avoiding direct contact with the offender. At social functions the situation becomes very uncomfortable. The shunned one is not permitted to eat with the members and is often relegated to a place far removed from the family unit. During the time the *Bann* is imposed the spouse and children of the offender are to have no interaction with that person, of any sort, including the normal marital relations. This places a tremendous burden on the family and has caused some serious and deep-seated psychological problems for those involved. However, the leaders of the Amish church are vehement in their justification of *Meidung*. They argue that the member has made a solemn vow with God to live in a prescribed way, and any deviation from that way of life must be severely punished. This is the only way, they contend, that their church can continue to function as the central feature of the lives of its members. Church rules supersede family ties when a member is excommunicated and is, in effect, disowned. A former Amishman who was shunned for more than fifty years because he joined a more liberal church says that, "Shunning works a little bit like an electric fence around a pasture with a pretty good fence charger on it."[8] The courts have become involved with the Amish community because of *Meidung* on several occasions through the years. In a famous case from 1947, the person who was shunned actually brought suit against four of the members of the church who had imposed the *Bann*. The case caused great concern among the Amish who normally refrain from any dealings with "English" laws and courts. The case involved an Amishman who joined a more liberal church that permitted automobile ownership because his small daughter, who had polio, needed to be taken for treatment each week, to a town 15 miles from their home. The offender claimed it was an economic necessity that he have his own car to be assured the little girl would receive the

---

[8]Donald B. Kraybill, The Riddle of Amish Culture, (Baltimore: The Johns Hopkins University Press, 1989), 117.

essential medical care. The sensational case drew the attention of the media and had gone on for more than three years before it was concluded. Although the jury awarded him $5,000.00 in damages, the defendants refused to pay. The farm of one of them was eventually sold at sheriff's sale and the ill will and suffering of all parties involved cannot be measured in dollars.

A recent Associated Press story relates the tale of Aaron S. Glick, of Lancaster County, Pennsylvania, who had been shunned nearly 50 years ago for using a tractor in his fields. He was placed under the *Bann* and has never been reinstated. He filed a complaint stating that Christ Stoltzfoos, a hardware store owner, and his employees who were also Amish, refused to accept payment for some hardware items purchased by Glick. The two men had already put some of their differences behind them, according to Glick. "Christ came out to my place last fall after there was a meeting of the Amish bishops," Glick said. "He apologized and told me that I could buy things but I still had to pay cash. No checks." Glick, 72, needs to pay by check so that he has receipts for tax purposes. The Pennsylvania Human Relations Commission ruled that Stoltzfoos "must cease and desist from the unlawful discriminatory practice of treating customers who have left the Old Order Amish differently than other customers who patronize Valley Hardware Store." "If the state rules that's the law, I'm sure he'll abide by it," Glick said of Stoltzfoos.[9]

The excommunicated Amish person is under a tremendous amount of pressure to confess, ask forgiveness and become reinstated in the church. This is the result desired by the officials when *Meidung* is imposed and it has the desired effect in many cases. Some people, however, are so sure of their innocence that they never go back and, thus, impose serious hardships upon their entire family and circle of friends. Some who have been excommunicated relocate and join more liberal churches to relieve the pressures of living within the community where the excommunication took place.

---

[9] "Store Owner Ordered to Treat Shunned Man as Regular Customer," The Herald, 28 July 94, 30.

Chapter 8
The Home and the Barn

To say that the Amish home is the heart of Amish family life would be a glaring understatement. Not only is the home the center of Amish life, it is the only place, other than the one-room schoolhouse, where the major ceremonies and events of life take place. There are no Amish church buildings...preaching services are held in the home and/or the barn. There are no Amish funeral homes...the viewing of the body and the religious service take place in the home. Although some Amish women do go to hospitals to give birth, many Amish children are born in the home. The Amish do not generally go to bowling alleys, skating rinks, arcades, movies or pizza shops or other retail entertainment facilities for their recreation. They play group games, board games, read or do crafts, at home, with their families, for diversion. The young people attend bees, frolics, singings and weddings, all held in Amish homes, during their courting years. There are no Amish nursing homes. The aged are revered and greatly respected and elderly family members remain in the family home as long as it is physically possible to care for them. Many Amish people who sense that their lives are nearing the end request the privilege of being allowed to die, with dignity, at home if at all possible. Throughout the rest of modern American society the family unit and the basic values associated with a strong family life have been seriously eroded. The family dinner hour, where the day's happenings are shared, has given way to the hectic schedules of two-paycheck families and the children's activities, all of which take place outside the home. The Amish family, by way of contrast, still sits down together at the table for two or three meals each day and because the farms or cottage industries provide much of the income and involve all of the family members, the family unit is preserved.

The Amish homes are not at all uniform in appearance. This is an apparent deviation from their strong belief in conformity as a means of avoiding pridefulness in members of the church community. Part of the explanation for this is that the Amish often occupy homes that were originally built by "English." But when they were first settling in the Lancaster County area of Pennsylvania, their homes did have a distinctive style. The following historical information on early Amish architecture is from the research of Stephen Scott:

> The houses were known as the Continental-style as it probably originated in Europe. The Amish term for this corridor-kitchen house is *Flurkuchenhaus* and is represented by the Herr house, built in 1719, one of the few surviving houses in this style. One of the features of this style is the central chimney and fireplace, with three rooms around it. This is in contrast with the British settlers who built their fireplaces in one end of the formal sitting room. Another unique char-acteristic of the early Amish home was that the fireplace opened into the *Kuch* (kitchen), which has always been the hub of Amish family life. The closed back of the fireplace was extended into the room opposite the *Kuch*, making a much more efficient use of the fuel used to heat the home. This room is known as the *Schtupp*, meaning "stove room," and much family activity took place here because of the warmth from the stove. The main entrance to the house and the closed stairways to the basement and the second floor also began in the *Kuch*.

A downstairs bedroom called the *Kammer* (chamber) was usually occupied by the father and mother. Some homes also had a small storage room or pantry called a *Kammerli* which was occasionally used as a bedroom if necessary.

As the Amish families grew and their farms became more prosperous, larger homes were needed. The roomier Georgian style homes which originated in England filled the bill and became plentiful in Amish communities. Georgian houses featured four nearly equal-sized rooms divided by a large central hallway containing the stairway to the second floor which also had four rooms. The facade was symmetrical, with a doorway in the center of the first floor, flanked by two identical windows on each side. there were five more of these windows evenly spaced along the second floor. Each gable end had a built in chimney and two windows on the first floor and two corresponding windows on the second floor.

As the years went by, these two styles were merged and the result was the Quaker-plan house or the two-thirds Georgian house or the Continental deep house. This style had an offset door to the first floor but the fireplace was in one of the gable ends rather than in the center of the floorplan.

Another variation of the combination was the house that appears to be the Georgian style from the outside but the inside retains the three-room floorplan. This is sometimes referred to as the Pennsylvania farmhouse by architectural historians. Many of these houses had two side-by-side front doors which has caused much speculation among those who study such details. A possible explanation is that one door was an everyday entrance to the kitchen while the other opened into the formal living room or parlor. This way visitors could be taken into the best part of the house without going through the lived-in quarters. A Lancaster County Amishman called the extra door a "boyfriend door" because the young men traditionally avoided the family of their girlfriend and this door provided the opportunity of going directly into the parlor where some evening dates took place.

Although the Amish have adopted more modern styles of architecture, the original names for the downstairs rooms are still used. The *Kuch* is still the kitchen, but is much larger now and may include the dining area and an informal living area. *Schtupp* no longer means "stove room," but is preceded by a descriptive adjective such as *gut Schtupp* (good room) or *schlof Schtupp* (sleep room). *Kammer* still designates a downstairs bedroom for the parents.[1]

Sometimes Amish families bought "English" farms and moved into the home already on the property. They would modify the structure to conform with the rules of the church community, which meant tearing out the electrical wiring, the plumbing and the telephone wires. If there was an open porch on the front or the back of the house, it would usually be closed in. If the house was any color but white, it would be painted. Any frivolous decorations on the outside of the house would be removed.

As the Amish families grew, so did their homes. There were additional bedrooms added to the original plan which had only two second floor bedrooms, one for boys and one for girls. Some

---

[1]Stephen Scott, <u>Amish Houses and Barns</u>, (Intercourse, Pennsylvania: Good Books, 1992), 14-17.

additional rooms were added on the first floor, as well. Often, a bedroom in addition to the *Kammer*, would be drawn into the first floor plan. As the Amish builders began to work outside of their communities and construct homes for non-Amish, some of their homes reflected those styles. Closets were added in the hallways and between rooms and storage areas were built into nooks and crannies in the first floor. The Old Order Amish home is constructed with removable walls between some of the first floor rooms. This allows for easy expansion of floor space for the preaching services and weddings and funerals, which traditionally are attended by several hundred family members and friends.

The kitchen, truly the center of the home and the life of the family, will be discussed in detail in the following chapter.

A most distinctive feature of the Amish homestead is the addition of a second, somewhat smaller, dwelling attached to the main house or built very close by. This is called the *Grossdaadi Haus* or granddaddy house, where the older generation lives after they have retired from the more demanding chores on the farm. The *Grossdaadi Haus*, if attached to the larger home, has its own entrance, living quarters and kitchen. Most of the meals are prepared and eaten separately from the rest of the extended family. This innovation allows the older generation the privacy needed to maintain a lifestyle of their own, but adds the security of having the other two or three generations close at hand if they are needed. The continuity of the family circle is maintained, as well. The younger family will gradually take over the responsibilities of running the farm while the grandparents continue to have input into the decisions and continue to help with the chores. As the younger folks become competent at the business of farming, the elders take a less and less active role in the everyday running of the farm. If they are actively involved in a shop of some sort, they continue to work, at their own pace. They become retired bit-by-bit and do not have the stress of dealing with the financial hardships many "English" retirees face. They are never made to feel useless in their society, because they gain respect as they age. Their opinions are valued and sought on issues in the church, as well as, other areas of their lives.

Living in such close proximity could lead to some conflicts unless the issues are talked about and dealt with before the situation gets out of hand. Adjustments are needed by all involved. The Amish are human, after all, and can have some of the same emotional upheavals as the members of society at large. One widow from an Amish community in Kansas has written, anonymously, of the relationship between the grandparents and the younger couple they share the farm with:

When we moved in at one end of the house with his parents, my husband and I already had a few children, and we made guidelines for ourselves.

Rule Number 1: Not to expect them to care for our children while we did the chores. My husband always said that they took care of their own children, so why bother them with ours. I made many a trip to the house during chores to check on them.

Rule Number 2: Don't expect Grandpa to come out to help with the field work.

Rule Number 3: If Grandma and Grandpa wanted a few chores to do as long as they were able, cooperate with them. So we had the chickens and hogs on a 50-50 basis. Each of us did a share of the work, with the cleaning of the houses always being our job. My husband and I always tried to do the heaviest part of the work.

Rule Number 4: Never get aggravated at Grandpas if they advise us how to be more saving. (Even though we felt we were already trying.) They started up farming in the early 1900's and we in the early 1940's.

Rule Number 5: Always pay our rent when

due. We knew that's what they depended on for their living, especially after Grandpa's health failed, so he had no share in doing chores anymore.

Rule Number 6: Never interfere with their plans if they want to go somewhere. Always be willing to hitch up a horse for them when they need one, even though they could have done it themselves.

Rule Number 7: Never expect them to care for your children so that you can go to the field, but we'd fix a special place at the head of the field for the little ones if the weather was nice.

Rule Number 8: Always be very appreciative if Grandma comes over to help with the work.

Rule Number 9: If the Grandparents ask you to do something for them, small tasks that they can't do anymore, always be sure to say, "You're welcome-I was glad to do it for you." This means so much to the Grandparents.

Rule Number 10: Never go to your brothers and sisters and complain about Grandpa and Grandma, especially after one is left alone. Try to work these things out between you in a nice way.

Rule Number 11: Realize that it costs Grandparents something to live, and if Grandma has taken in quilting or quilt piecing to supplement their income, take an interest in her work and respect her for it. Even though you don't have time to help (she doesn't expect it.) Just let her know you care and love her.[2]

Besides the house and its added *Grossdaadi Haus*, the Amish farms must have numerous outbuildings to house the animals

---

[2]A Widow in Kansas (1985): 4-5, in John A. Hostetler, <u>Amish Roots: A Treasury of History, Wisdom and Lore</u>, (Baltimore: The Johns Hopkins University Press, 1989), 97-98.

and store the grains or shops to provide a place to work in one of the many cottage industries now being pursued by the Amish. A wash house is a necessity because they are not permitted to go to the laundromat to do their laundry, but must do it at home. The wash house may be a small building adjacent to the house or, it may be attached to the house, near the kitchen. Either way, this little building provides a place for the water to be heated, for the washing to be done and for the washing machine to be stored when it is not in use. They use a gasoline engine to power a ringer-type washer and all the laundry is done on one day, usually Monday. There are, of course, no clothes dryers, but all of the washing is hung outside on clotheslines to dry. If the family is part of a very conservative Old Order Amish community the water will have to be pumped and carried, in large wash tubs, to the washer. Very often the woodshed is attached to the house near the kitchen and wash house, obviously, so the wood does not have to be carried far to the woodstove where the cooking is done and the water is heated for the washing machine.

If the family raises hogs and/or chickens, the pens for these creatures will also be on the property, but some distance away from the house. Other buildings found on the farm would be one (or more) machinery sheds, a buggy shed, a silo, a corncrib and other grain storage buildings, an outhouse, (unless the family belongs to a more liberal church community which allows indoor plumbing) a repair shop, or shop for creating products to be marketed, perhaps a windmill and, if this is a dairy farm, a barn and a milkhouse. The Amish have typically built the forebay or "Swiss" barn on their farms. There has been a great deal of study and confusion concerning the issue of the Pennsylvania barns. The forebay style is unique in that state. According to Robert F. Ensminger, "In spite of the practical value afforded by a forebay, extra space above and protection below, most barns in North America do not have them. Even the large two and a half story barns which occur from southern Quebec through upstate New England and from New York to Wisconsin lack the forebay.

Practical need did not influence the utilization of a forebay in these examples. However, banks, bridges and ramps for second floor access are consistently found in these as well as Pennsylvania Barns. It is a common error to use the term "bank barn" when referring to the Pennsylvania Barn. Although Pennsylvania Barns usually have ramps or are built against banks, so do many other types. But only the Pennsylvania Barn has a forebay."[3] Although some scholars disagree slightly, the bulk of the research suggests that the origin of the Pennsylvania Barn was in Europe, in the Palatine region of Switzerland, in the middle Rhine Valley. This is not a surprising conclusion, as that is precisely where the Old Order Amish originated. The early Swiss structures were a combination house and barn. The barn, stable and home were all under one roof and had a projected roof and a balcony above the stable entrance. The balcony floor provided the roof over the area below, where the cattle could be put in and out of the stable. The main part of the barn contained two grain storage ares on either side and a threshing floor in the center. The home occupied the top one or two stories of the structure. This basic style was apparently adapted by the Amish when they arrived on the shores of the New World and began to build their homes and barns. For the most part, the house and barn were constructed as two separate buildings and the barn was made in a style similar to the ones in their homeland. The stable on the ground floor, or basement, has rows on either side for the dairy cattle and an open area between the rows. There are compartments for grain storage in the ends, as well. The second floor is for hay storage and has large lofts and compartments for hay, straw and grain storage on either side of the entrance. Between the lofts is the threshing floor which also is used for machinery storage. The large double doors are on the ramp or "bank" side and the forebay is on the opposite, or downhill, side. The forebay is the length of the barn and is made by extending the beams of the threshing floor anywhere from ten to twenty feet, to make a

[3]Robert F. Ensminger, "A Search For the Origin of the Pennsylvania Barn," Pennsylvania Folklife 30 (Winter 1980-81): 51.

cantilevered arrangement above the stable doors. These barns are called "Swisser barns" or *Schweitzer Scheier* to this day. The very early Pennsylvania Barns were made from logs and, later, from wood that had been sawed into boards to cover the structure. The first floor, or foundation walls were built from stones taken from the fields on the farm. This is the predominant style of the barns erected by the early Amish as they arrived in southeastern Pennsylvania, and continues to be the preferred type at this time.

The interior of an Amish home is, as one would expect, quite simply furnished and decorated. As is true with every detail of their existence, the bishop and other church leaders have the final word on what is permitted and what is not. The variations in customs are also the result of the different degrees of conservatism within each church community. The following description attempts to take into consideration all of the differences from community to community. The walls are painted a pale blue, gray or green and the windows are either bare, have a single panel of black or white fabric pulled to one side or have dark window blinds. The livingroom floors are bare wood, waxed to a sheen, with homemade rag throw rugs under each of several rockers. The rockers will have been made by a member of the family or of the community and will probably be of oak and hickory or walnut and hickory. Other furniture includes a wooden armed settee, some straight-backed chairs and the treadle sewing machine, with which the Amish mother and her daughters make all of the family's clothing except their shoes, hats and some of their underwear. There will also be one or two plain wooden dressers or chests, sometimes a china cupboard and a bookcase. Some "fancy" dishes are permitted and may be displayed in the china cupboard or on the top of a chest. There are kerosene lanterns hanging at intervals from hooks in the ceiling and, perhaps, sitting on one or more of the chests, depending on the activities of the evening and where the light is needed. A clock shelf adorns nearly every Amish livingroom wall and, besides the wind-up clock, will also hold several pieces of decorative china or knickknacks. The clock will always be on Standard Time, never set ahead to conform with the "English" Daylight Savings Time. A hanging newspaper rack is also on most Amish livingroom walls to hold some of the favorite reading material of the family. Wooden pegs for hats and coats are along the wall, taking the place of closets. There are no mirrors, photographs or paintings on the wall. The only pictures that are displayed are the ones accompanied by a calendar, and there are usually several of them hanging here and there. The Amish ban on photographs is a result of their interpretation of the second commandment, Exodus 20:4, "Thou shalt not make unto thee any graven image, or any likeness of anything that is in heaven above, or that is in the earth beneath, or that is in the water under the earth." The Amish feel that a photo is a "likeness" and is, therefore, forbidden. Along with this rule is the fear that having one's pictures and mirrors to peer at could lead to false pride among the members. The reason for conformity and lack of individualism is to preserve the feeling of humility, group identity and *Gelassenheit*. Nobody in the Amish community deserves or gets more recognition than anyone else.

The *Kammer* is furnished with a double bed, a small table to hold the lantern, a dresser and pegs or hooks along the walls from which to hang clothes. There will also be a porcelain "chamber pot" under the bed, used on cold winter nights to avoid the long trek to the outhouse. The bedrooms on the second floor are for the children and are usually as sparsely furnished as the rest of the house. There are enough beds for the boys in one room and enough beds in the other room for the girls. One or more dressers or chests of drawers will be present to hold their folded clothing and these rooms, like the others downstairs, have wall hooks or pegs instead of closets. There is no heat in the second floor bedrooms, so they are for sleeping only, not for lounging and playing, as the bedrooms of the "English" children often are.

The lack of electricity in the Old Order Amish home is one of the most amazing features of their lifestyle. For the non-Amish person the thought of life without electricity is nearly unthinkable. We plug in literally dozens of appliances and gadgets in our homes and consider it a great hardship when there is a power outage and we must forego the convenience of flipping a switch. The Amish are opposed to electricity on the basis of their strong belief in remaining separate from the world. The scriptures provide several references to this doctrine. The words of I John 2:15 tell us to "Love not the world, neither the things that are in the world. If any man love the world, the love of the Father is not in him." Also, in John 17:14 Jesus said, "I have given them thy word; and the world hath hated them, because they are not of the world, even as I am not of the world," and in II Cor. 6:17, we are admonished, "Wherefore come out from among them, and be ye separate, saith the Lord, and touch not the unclean thing; and I will receive you." The Amish live by the Bible and its teachings and these verses emphasize the importance of being apart from those who are worldly. The use of electricity from power plants and from the lines strung all over the landscape would, undoubtedly, result in more involvement with the outside world. But, it was not without internal conflict that this conclusion was reached among the Old Order Amish. In the early days of electric power, the Amish had not developed a firm opinion on its use. They were generally opposed to using the electricity from the power plants, but were a bit more lenient on the question of using battery power. They reasoned that batteries were self-contained and did not hook them up with the outside world. In 1910. Isaac Glick was able to come up with an electric light using a generator. He used the light to check the fertility of eggs in his hatchery and was not reprimanded by the church. Then, he used his generator to light his barn and was censured this time. Glick was quick to abandon the light, but other Amish farmers were also using their batteries to power light bulbs in their barns. Meanwhile, the Peachy Amish (who had split with the Old Order

Amish as a result of a major controversy) were welcoming the new invention of electric power into their lives. This fact made the decision on electric use a bit easier for the Amish. If they were using it, it was to be banned by the more conservative group. Helping the decision-making were three episodes in the Amish community during 1919. Donald Kraybill reports that the first was concerning a tinsmith known as "Tinker" Dan Beiler who had a gasoline engine to run some of his tools. He was able to rig up a lightbulb which flickered with the speed of the generator. Many folks dropped by to see the contraption and the bishop, Ben Beiler, was not pleased. He ruled that the light was a step too far and would not waver. "Tinker" Dan Beiler was also vehement, and left the community to go to Virginia. Another Amishman, Ike Stoltzfus, had bought a generator to use in his greenhouse business and hooked up an electric pump to water his vegetable plants. Bishop Ben Beiler, the same Ben Beiler who ruled in the "Tinker" Dan case, ruled that the pump had to go. There were those who felt that the bishop "...just clamped down on him without taking it up with the church. Ike didn't know it was wrong, but the bishop, in his mind, thinks this member here was always kicking over the traces and his attitude isn't too good toward the church and we just can't tolerate this. So they gave Ike several weeks to get rid of it." And, he did. The third incident involved a man, Mike Stoltzfus, who used power tools in his buggy shop. Again, bishop Beiler said, "No," to the use of electricity. Mike was willing to go along with the ruling, even though some members felt that bishop Beiler "...was very influential on this electric question, in setting the direction, definitely. With another bishop it might have gone a different direction. It probably would have. At least the people would have been able to help make the decision. He was pretty much making the decisions and not taking them to a vote in the congregation." Nevertheless, the ban on electricity was in place and has held.[4]

---

[4]Donald B. Kraybill, The Riddle of Amish Culture, (Baltimore: The Johns Hopkins University Press 1989), 152-153.

The church leaders did, however, continue to permit the use of the 12-volt batteries to power motors and flashlights. The ban on electricity was not really challenged again until the 1960's when the horse-drawn farm machinery was scarce and the Amish farmers were beginning to use the generators and electric welders. The bishops were tolerant of this as long as it was used to adapt and repair the machinery used with horses. Then the controversy arose again in the late 1960's when milk companies were demanding that the farmers store and chill their milk in large stainless steel tanks. The church leaders had been permitting the dairy farmers to cool the milk in coolers powered by diesel engines, but this was a different issue. Not wishing to thwart the efforts of the farmers and deprive them of their primary source of income, the bishops had a predicament on their hands. The milk companies had standards of sanitation and nutrition to maintain, but they need the Amish farmers' product. The negotiations got underway and were complicated by two major problems, besides the electricity issue. They required that the milk be stirred periodically to prevent the cream from rising to the top, which meant 110-volt current was needed to run the agitator. In addition, they wanted to pick up the milk every day of the week, including Sundays, a violation of their belief that no business could be transacted on the sabbath. The milk companies and the bishops reached a compromise. The agitation mechanisms were to be powered by the diesel engines and the generators could be used to charge their batteries. On the issue of Sunday pick-up, there was no room for compromise. The Amish leaders would absolutely not permit it. The milk companies were forced to concede. They adjusted their route schedules to pick up very late on Saturday evenings, just before midnight.[5]

The telephone is another taboo instrument of the "English" world, although they were used early in this century when they were new and novel. According to one source, an Amishman

---

[5]Kraybill, 156-159

said, of the telephone, "I remember when the phones came. The church didn't say anything about them. It was thumbs up. Two of my wife's uncles had the phones in and there were quite a few others that had them, then an issue came up. Two people talking on the phone were gossiping about someone else and it went so far that it became a church issue. They were asked to come to church and make a confession about it. Then the church decided that it was just better not to allow these phones." Although there is no real scriptural reference to the use of such a device, the *Ordnung* forbade it around 1910 on the basis that it allowed too much interaction with the worldly "English" and undermined the Amish attempt to remain a separate society.[6] However, phone usage is permitted in emergency situations and the church leadership has no problem with the phone on that basis. Many Amish folks use their neighbors' telephones or a wayside phone booth. Some of these rural telephone booths have a hitching post or rail nearby to make it easier for the Amish patrons to avail themselves of the phone. As the telephone became more and more evident in modern society, there were changes made within the Amish church to compromise and permit easier access to the instrument. Phone shanties, very similar to outhouses, are allowed in some communities. These small buildings house a telephone which is paid for and used by several Amish farm families. They are placed away from the house and do not have a loud bell. The requirement for an unlisted number is strictly enforced, allowing the Amish farmer to conduct his business, but avoiding the direct link with the outside world that a published phone number offers.[7] So, once again, the Amish church leaders have had to wrestle with a problem of modern technology and have reached a reasonable compromise. The telephone is unconditionally forbidden in the Old Order Amish home, but its use is allowed on a strictly limited basis. This arrangement is satisfactory as it gives the Amish

---

[6]Kraybill, 143.
[7]Kraybill, 144.

community access to phones when absolutely necessary without jeopardizing the teachings of the Bible and the rules of the *Ordnung*.

Although the structure and the interior decoration of the Amish home is very simple and unadorned, the lawn and gardens surrounding these homes are very often spectacular showcases of blossoms and bounty. The flower and vegetable gardens appear in virtually every Amish yard, regardless of whether the family makes its living by farming, or not. The flower garden is sometimes a self-contained bed of annuals and perennials or may be a series of rows in the vegetable garden. In addition to the flowers planted in beds, there are the ones that give decorative touches all over the yards. The outhouse is usually surrounded on three sides by a perennial such as hollyhocks or an annual like morning glories. There will likely be climbing roses on trellises at the edges of the yard and, often, the mailbox post is surrounded by a colorful array of flowers. The flowers afford the Amish women a bright and showy expression of their personalities that is forbidden in all other aspects of their life. The flowers are God's handiwork, they reason, so they cannot be denied.

The Amish family is a closely woven unit and the resulting fabric is a strong one. The home is central to the lives of an Amish family and is an attitude as much as it is a physical structure. One unidentified Amish woman writes of the meaning of home and Amish life:

I am Rich

Home is a place to relax. It need not be a fancy structure or modern. It is not just a place to eat or drink or to change clothes like a filling station. It can be a harbor of peace--if the Lord is permitted inside.

In our home we have no running water. A pump at the kitchen sink furnishes all the water we care to use. We have no skin problems, for with our silky rain water, we need no detergents. When getting dinner for company, we never have to stop and run to the basement because the pressure is way down. There is very little expense involved in our water system, just an occasional change of leather and that requires no mechanical ability. As for hot water, we have our old reliable teakettle. For heating wash water, we use the iron kettle and feel it is a luxury because in many parts of the world people do their laundry in the creeks.

Heating? We have no central system, not even an enameled stove. All we have is the same black model which for many is only a childhood memory. When coming inside, how comfortable it is to warm our chilling fingers. Where else could we toast our feet so satisfactorily and feel the warmth seep upward through the veins? Of course it must be fed and in zero or sub-zero temperatures it is a starving creature. But with the basement filled with wood, which the members of our family have labored so generously to provide for us, what more could we ask? When I look at the racks of wood, I feel humbly grateful for I know that in the world, many people are cold, living in huts, without even a blanket.

We have no padded or overstuffed seats to sit down upon. All we have are lightweight hickory rockers and they are so portable. If we need more light we carry one to the window, if we're cold we carry it to the stove and prop up our feet in a very un-lady-like manner on the nickel trimmings of our stove. If someone comes with a baby, the rocker can be moved to the bedroom for there it is quiet. When it comes to entertainment we have the very best. Mother Nature is our Master Performer--the beauty of bare branches etched in front of a colorful sunset. I wonder how many people ever notice the varying branch formations on different trees. The cool colors of a winter sunrise are often overlooked by sleepy eyes. The ever-changing sky always has something interesting to see. The fluffy clouds of summer, the turbulence of a windy day in spring, or a heavy snowfall in winter, each season has its attractions.

In our leisure time we often watch our little feathered friends. It is a thrifty form of entertainment with a home-made bird feeder and home-grown sunflower and squash seeds and corn. How exciting to see our first evening grosbeak! The pileated woodpecker may be as homely as a mudpie but it is still a rare sight to behold. The saucy chickadee darts between the suet and feeder almost faster than the eye can see. Even some kinds of our lowly sparrows are very attractive.

For real excitement on the farm, there's nothing like gathering the first egg from a flock of chickens you've raised from baby chicks. Nor is there anything as tasty as vegetables you've hoed and cultivated till you're hot and tired. When we stop to consider, it's nothing short of a miracle when we behold how much God provides for us to eat, all from one little dried-up dead-looking seed.

No, we have no so-called modern conveniences, but we are blessed with an abundance of life's necessities. We don't have an overflowing grocery cart, or beautiful clothes or a big bank account to fall back on.

But I do have a family and friends, and many people I meet on life's highway. I have good eyesight, a healthy mind and body. **I AM RICH.**

May I remember to be as rich with gratitude as I am rich with gifts which God has bestowed upon me.[8]

---

[8]Joe Wittmer, <u>The Gentle People: Personal Reflections of Amish Life</u>, (Minneapolis, Minnesota: Educational Media Corporation, 1991), 41-43.

Chapter 9
The Amish Kitchen

If the home is the very center of Amish life, then the kitchen is the very center of that home. The kitchen table is the gathering place for the family as they partake of the meals so lovingly prepared in the kitchen. It is the place where the scholars do their studies on cold winter evenings and it is the center of activities and board games when friends and family come to visit after the chores are finished. The farm and the barn are the Amish farmer's domain and the house and lawn are his wife's. Her role is clearly defined within the Amish culture and there is little chance of change. The women's liberation movement of several decades ago has had virtually no impact on the Amish woman. She marries for life, taking a vow that is between herself, her husband and God and it is expected that the couple will live a Christian life together and forgive the faults of their partner. There is no public expression of affection between men and women as it is believed that this is an unnecessary display of emotion and is just not appropriate for Amish couples. Amish women are fully aware of their role in the society as they are brought up learning, at their mother's side, what is expected of them. It is clearly defined in the Bible in I Cor. 11:3, "But I would have you know, that the head of every man is Christ; and the head of the woman is the man..." Because the scriptures are taken quite literally by the Amish there is no room for deviation. She is not subservient to her husband, however, and has an equal role in making decisions that affect the entire family. Her husband will consult her when such need arises and together they will make the decision. She has the last word in most lesser decisions which involve the home and their daily lives. The Biblical edict that the man is the head of the woman does not mean that abuse and harshness are present in the marriage. The husband, while he does not openly praise or compliment his wife, has a deep and lasting respect for her and the role she plays in his life and that of their children. She has a vote in church council, but does not have the opportunity to serve in any of the leadership roles. Her first loyalty is to God, and if her husband sins and is placed under the ban, then she must shun him according to the *Ordnung*. She is the primary disciplinarian in the home, but when he is at home, the children's father is also responsible for correcting any behavior problems. During some seasons and in some situations, the wives do go to the fields or to the shop to help their husbands with the excess work, but they are not expected to do so if there is an extra heavy load of work to be done in the house or garden. Most Amish wives are fulfilled by their life's work of caring for a home and raising children and few of them work out, away from home. One young Amish woman, married ten years and with five children ranging in age from three months through nine years, put it like this, "It would break me in pieces if I would have to put my children into a day care center to go to work. The children need their mother at home to give them love, understanding, teaching and discipline while they are growing up. Do you really think those children will go to the parents with their problems when they couldn't be with them to discuss their problems when they were little?"[1] Many Amish women do have a separate source of income and that is theirs to do with as they wish. This income usually comes from selling eggs or produce at the roadside or from selling quilts and hand-crafted items to shops that are patronized by tourists. Because the farm is the source of income for many Amish families, the barn and machinery have been modernized more

[1]Alma Hershberger, <u>Amish Women</u>, (Dansville, Ohio: Art of Amish Taste, 1992), 56-57.

rapidly than the kitchen. Even though there are some technological improvements, like synthetic fabrics that require much
less work and powerful cleansers and detergents, some of the
women are of the opinion that the men have the edge when it
comes to labor-saving devices. One anonymous Amishwoman
stated her feelings like this:

> The joke among us women is that the men
> make the rules so that's why more modern things
> are permitted in the barn than in the house. The
> women have no say in the rules. Actually, I think
> the main reason is the men make the living and we
> don't make a living in the house. So you have to go
> along with what they need out there. You know,
> if the public health law calls for it, you have to have
> it. In the house you don't. Even my dad says he
> thinks the Amishwomen get the brunt of it all
> around. They have so many children and are
> expected to help out with the milking. Some help
> for two hours with the milking from beginning to
> end and they have five little children. That's all
> right if a man helps them in the house and puts the
> children to bed, but a lot of them don't. I don't
> think it's fair that we have the push mowers to
> mow the lawns with. It's hard work on some of
> these lawns. We keep saying that if the men would
> mow the lawns they would have motors on them,
> and I am sure there would be. Years ago they used
> to mow the hay fields with an old horse mower,
> but now they have engines on the field mowers so
> it goes easier for the horses, but they don't care
> about the women.[2]

This is not to suggest that the Amish women, as a whole, are

---

[2]Donald B. Kraybill, The Riddle of Amish Culture, (Baltimore: The Johns Hopkins University Press, 1989), 73.

discontented. They accept, with humility, the role carved out for them in their society and gain satisfaction from the fruits of their labors and of their loins. When asked about the duties of an Amish wife, one woman answered, "I don't feel like I have duties as a wife or a mother. Duties are something that you have to do. I am not forced to do anything that I do not want to do. It is my choice to be a mother and a wife. I feel that this is a privilege that God gave me a loving husband. My husband doesn't ask much of me as far as helping him with his work in the woodwork shop. I try to keep the children and the house so it may be pleasant for him. For a mother and a wife who stays home, it brings much fulfillment to me, to make a house a home."[3]

Because food preparation and preservation take up the bulk of the Amish wife's time, the kitchen is the heart of her domain and is the place she spends most of her hours. The Amish kitchen is large room and has enough space for a long table, benches and chairs to accommodate all of the immediate family members, as well as all of the other things needed to prepare food for the family. There is a sink with a hand pump, in the very strict Old Order communities, or faucets to turn on the water which is stored in a holding tank and runs by gravity. The cookstove takes up a large amount of space and the wood-burning ones are used for both cooking and heat. During the frosty winter months, the kitchen is the warmest room in the house. The children are always in a hurry to get out of toasty, warm beds, run through the frigid bedroom and head down-stairs to the warmth of the kitchen to get dressed. It is a woodstove in the Old Order kitchen, but may be powered by propane in the more progressive communities. Usually, a rocker or couch is nearby for those rare moments of relaxation after dinner. Because of the lack of electricity in the Amish home, there are few appliances. The liberal communities that permit propane to be used as a fuel may also allow the use of refrigerators and freezers that run on "bottled gas." Even these more

---

[3]Hershberger, 56.

liberal homes are without many of the amenities we moderns are used to and seem to belong in a century past. The kitchen is a practical work area and has functional cabinets and cupboards. Often a "Hoosier cupboard," a free-standing cabinet with flour and sugar bins in the top and drawers and a large storage area below. Between the top and bottom of the cabinet is a large porcelain or zinc counter for rolling out dough and other food preparation. Between the counter surface and the top of the cabinets where flour and sugar are stored, is a storage area behind a rolltop or cupboard doors and often has a built-in spice rack in that section. These cabinets are sought by "English" collectors of antiques, but are sought by the Amish as a needed work space and storage area. There are shelves on the kitchen walls, where some of the "fancy" dishes are displayed and a matchbox holder hangs above the stove. On the countertops there may be an old-fashioned, Amish-made cylinder churn, made of wood or a more modern one "...built for demanding, continuous use. Tough nylon dasher and indestructible plastic jar. Fully enclosed and lubricated cast gears turn smoothly dirt-free and safe from stray fingers. 14 1/4" holds 5 qt. churns 3 qt., 4 lbs.," according to Lehman's Non-Electric Catalog, published by Lehman Hardware and Appliances in Kidron, Ohio.[4] This catalog offers a plethora of necessities for the Amish home. The Lehman Hardware Store was established in 1919 and served both Amish and "English" families in the rural community surrounding Kidron. As technology improved and the old-fashioned things they sold were outdated, the owners of the store continued to stock the less modern items that were becoming more and more difficult to locate. They have an amazing array of household and hardware items from the early years of the twentieth century. The merchandise is new, repro-duced to fit a rural, non-electric lifestyle. The store covers more than an acre of floorspace and boasts the East's largest collection of cookstoves. There are more than 80 types which burn wood

---

[4]Lehman's Non-Electric Catalog, (Kidron, Ohio: n.p., n.d.), 3.

or gas or have been electrified for the non-Amish customer. The catalog lists more than 2,000 items, including nine pages of non-electric lamps and accessories, 21 pages of housewares and cookware and four pages of washday supplies.

The cooking pots are always quite large and are of cast iron, granite ware or aluminum. The utensils are also large enough to stir and scrape the over-sized kettles and serving dishes. A teakettle often sits atop the cookstove, keeping a supply of hot water on hand for doing dishes. The "dishwashers" are the children, who take turns washing and drying the family's dishes and pots and pans after the meal. The hot water from the stove is handled by the mother or one of the older girls and is poured into the basins used for washing and rinsing.

All of the organizational skills needed to efficiently run the Amish home may be a bit overwhelming to the young, newly-married Amish girl, even if she was raised to help her mother. One of the publications read by Amish young people, "Young Companion," has featured an article written by an anonymous thirty-five year old "experienced" housewife. The piece is aimed at the young married woman and offers some very practical hints on the fine art of washing dishes.

"Advice For the Young Married Woman"

There are a number of tricks to make the old-fashioned way easier, more efficient and more enjoyable.

To begin with, people who have no other stove to cook with except a wood stove, heat their dishwater while they are cooking the meal. This way the fire is not needed for so long. Also, they use the "summer wood" which burns quickly, heats well in the process, then dries out. Be sure to heat enough hot water to refill the dishpan if there are a lot of dishes. Washing dishes in cold water is not fun, and it does a poor job.

Once the meal is past, the dishes, pots, pans, platters and bowls are stacked with the largest at the bottom. A cabinet top near the dry sink serves as counter space and so does a deep window sill or a table.

Next, put the chunk of homemade soap in the dishpan and pour the hot water over it. (You should use rain water. Hard water doesn't work.) This will produce nice suds, especially if you're using a new chunk of soap. In fact, you will have to remove the soap before very long or you will have far too many suds.

These suds are so different from detergent suds. Detergent suds are all on top. The suds of homemade soap are mixed in *and* on top of the water, making it nice and soft. Too many suds make the water slippery and slithery, or even slimy. I remember having to scoop suds out by the handful and still there were too many, all because I had left the soap in too long.

But, when your chunk is old and small, you can pour hot water over it, swish all you like, and still get barely enough suds. Then it is time for a new chunk of soap.

An inbetween chunk of soap can be left in the water for a while, then removed for a turn, and when the suds grow fewer, put back into the water. Only don't forget to take the soap out before you dump the water. Otherwise you will have to look for it in the grass and pick off any dirt and blades of grass that stick to it, or give it a good rinse at the pump.

If you have now done all the dishes, please wipe out the sink before you dump the water.

You'll want to wring the 'sink' water into the dishpan. And before you hang up the dishrag, rinse it in clean water. This will help to keep it from getting slippery.

When every dish has been put away, the sink is dry, the dishpan empty, and the dishrag hung up--how tidy the kitchen looks. And the dishpan can be used to snitz apples, scrub carrots, peel potatoes, you name it.

I'm not yet thirty-five, but I still prefer the old-fashioned way, especially the homemade soap.[5]

The vegetable garden is one of the Amish wife's responsibilities and it provides almost all of the family's fresh produce during the summer and canned vegetables during the winter. The garden is usually quite large, as much as 1/6 of an acre and requires an enormous amount of time to plant and care for. But they are always near an Amish home, even non-farm homes, and embody more than just a source of food for the family. The garden provides a ready-made teaching tool for the youngsters in the family. The Amish virtues of family togetherness, self-sufficiency and independence are all represented as every family member, even the very small children, are given tasks to do in the garden. The children are taught consistency and perseverance and gain a sense of accomplishment from the work they do and observe others doing in the garden, season after season.[6] Early in the spring, as soon as the ground has thawed enough to work it, the garden chores are begun. The husband and wife will often be seen together working manure into the soil and plowing the ground. The first seeds to be sowed are the peas, which go in next to the perennials that are in the outside rows. These are asparagus, rhubarb and strawberries, along with some of the

---

[5]Joe Wittmer, The Gentle People: Personal Reflections of Amish Life, (Minneapolis, Minnesota: Educational Media Corporation, 1991), 90-91.
[6]Bernadette Hutchison, "Amish Gardens: A Symbol of Identity," Pennsylvania Folklife 43 (Spring 1994): 137.

decorative flowers that are almost always planted at the edge of the garden. The rest of the garden is planted in stages and the vegetables are rotated each year to preserve the soil's nutrients. Some of the vegetables are planted more than once to ensure a continuous supply throughout the growing season. By early June the garden is all in and the children wait, excitedly, for the first little green shoots to poke through the dirt. As the plants grow, so do the weeds and the bugs come. The small children are taught to pick the insects off the plants and the older ones are learning to wield the cultivator or the hoe. Before long, the first crops are ready to be enjoyed and, if appropriate, put up for winter.

The canning and preserving of food is at its peak in summer and autumn when the vegetables from the kitchen garden and the fruits from the orchard are being harvested. The women and girls of the family are busy from dawn to past dark with these chores, in addition to all of the other things they must do. Often, a frolic or sisters' day will be held to get the canning done if a family is having difficulty getting it finished while the harvest is at its best. The summer kitchen is a small room or building attached to the main house, just off the kitchen, where much of the cooking and canning are accomplished during the warm months. Some of the root crops, such as potatoes, beets, turnips, carrots and onions, are not canned, but are stored in a cool part of the basement or in the root cellar, a room dug out of the foundation for this purpose. The shelves full of hundreds of jars of canned fruits, vegetables, jellies, jams and pickles and a full root cellar are the rewards of the hours of toil in the kitchen or summer kitchen.

Amish women have won the admiration of "English" women and men for their tireless efforts to make their home a happy and loving one. One non-Amish man observer was so impressed by their "simplicity, their food preparation, and their cooking" that he penned this description of their daily lives as a tribute to them:

Amish women are hard workers. They start

when they are small children and by the time they get married they have picked up all of the essential housekeeping and farming skills that make them such a valuable economic asset in the Amish community...

The kitchen is the center for Amish family life. The kitchen table is where everybody eats. Sometimes there is oilcloth on the table, most often it is bare. There is no table linen although cupboards sometimes have inside shelves draped with folded paper napkins. Regular dishes are plain heavy china, sometimes picked up at an auction. Utensils are usually stainless steel, never silver. Some families have brightly colored dishes and other pretty things displayed even though "pride and vanity" are outlawed. Painted tomato cans and clay pots are placed on window sills, a riot of flowering plants inside brighten up the kitchen. Occasional embroidered pieces are also colorful and charming.

Plain single blind draped curtains, blue or green, are found in many windows, but a large number of the older families have no curtains at all.

The stricter families have historically used coal stoves and kerosene or oil lamps. Propane and natural gas, some of it produced on Amish farmland, is now used by more liberal amish districts. Thousands of mantels burn in gas lit homes along the main and country back roads. Gas stoves and ovens abound, and there are even homes with central heating systems here and there. But fine quilts filled with wool and heavy blankets and comforters are depended on more than central plants.

There are plenty of outhouses as part of the

country landscape, although many families have added more sophisticated plumbing in recent years. Tub baths, once common and sometimes communal, have been in some cases replaced by fixed bathtubs and showers as water systems have been developed that are acceptable to various groups. Clothing is hand-washed and sun- and wind-dried in summer and winter.

There is little time for back fence gossiping and coffee-klatching in the Amish woman's day. She makes her own clothes (except for shoes and simple underwear) and also makes workclothes for the men in the family as well as all the children's clothing. She is sometimes a barber and a doctor, bandaging up the cuts and abrasions that are everyday problems on the working farm. She is constantly mending and fixing the house; there is always something to be done.

It would be a serious mistake, however, to think that there is not a lot of joy and happiness in an Amish home because of the constant work and never ending responsibilities built into raising such large families in severe surroundings. Most Amish women love flowers and there are always patches of colorful geraniums and marigolds, mixed with nasturtiums at times, decorating Amish lawns. There are apple-paring parties and auctions, town trips and visits, church Sundays and family reunions, barn raisings to cook for, and weddings galore. There are Amish women who play baseball and frisbee with enthusiasm and great style. At the other extreme, Amish mothers read Bible stories in German to their little children with great reverence and feeling...

Amish women do not use cosmetics. They usually don't

have to. The rosy cheeks of the Amish and their fine clear skin, often freckled, needs no enhancing. They are naturally good-looking people, vigorous and healthy women playing roles prescribed for them by tradition, maintained by perseverance, and apparently more than satisfying their needs for a complete and dedicated life.[7]

There are literally hundreds and hundreds of favorite Amish dishes, and many of the recipes have been handed down through the generations from the Jura Mountains and the Palatine region of Switzerland. The Old Order Amish do, now and then, use mixes and a few prepared foods, but they normally make the dishes served in their homes from "scratch." Although it is not possible to print even a fraction of them in this work, a representative sample of Amish favorites has been included. There are old, traditional dishes which are used on special occasions and everyday fare which is in every Amish woman's repertoire. Some of the recipes have been adapted to reflect the changes in food preservation and availability.

Though the widespread myth that the Amish housewife always serves seven sweets and seven sours, is just that, a myth, there are lots of pickled goodies in the pantry of the Amish home.

Chow chow is a favorite "sour" addition to the main meal which is eaten alone or as a sauce on meats. Its ingredients vary, depending on availability and preference within the home. The following is a typical recipe for **CHOW CHOW:**

> 1/4 peck (2 qts.) green beans
> 1 large head cauliflower, separated into flowerets
> 3 cups shelled lima beans
> 3 cups fresh whole kernel corn
> 1 qt. onions, chopped
> 5 green peppers, chopped
> 1/4 peck (2 qts.) green tomatoes, chopped

---

[7]Bill Randle, "Amish Women and Their Kitchens," in Amish Roots: A Treasury of History, Wisdom and, Lore, John A. Hostetler, ed., (Baltimore: The Johns Hopkins University Press, 1989), 101-102.

3 qts. cider vinegar
4 cups sugar
1/2 cup salt
2 Tbl. celery seed
2 Tbl. yellow mustard seed
2 Tbl. dry mustard
1 Tbl. turmeric

Cut the beans into 1/2 inch pieces. Cook green beans, cauliflowerets, lima beans and corn separately in boiling water until just tender. Drain. Mix the onions, peppers and tomatoes with the cooked vegetables in a large heavy kettle. Bring the vinegar to boiling and stir in a mixture of sugar, salt, celery seed, mustard seed, dry mustard and turmeric. Pour vinegar mixture over vegetables, bring to a boil and cook 20-25 minutes, or until thoroughly heated, stirring occasionally. Pour into sterilized jars and seal. Makes about 12 pints.[8]

This sweet pickle recipe takes some planning ahead
SEVEN DAY SWEET PICKLES...

1st day-Wash 7 lbs. medium sized green cucum-
bers   and cover with <u>boiling</u> water.

2nd day-Drain. Cover with fresh boiling water.

3rd day-Repeat second day.

4th day-Repeat second day.

5th day-Cut pickles into 1/4 inch rings.

Combine:

         1 qt. white vinegar
         8 cups granulated sugar
         2 Tbl. salt
         2 Tbl. mixed pickle spices

Bring to a full boil and pour over sliced pickles.

6th day-Drain brine from pickles, bring to a full boil

---

[8]Lillie S. Lustig, ed., <u>Pennsylvania Dutch Cookbook of Fine Old Recipes</u>, (Reading, Pennsylvania: Culinary Arts Press, 1967), 61.

and pour over pickles again.

7th day-Repeat same as 6th day. Jar and seal.[9]

Coleslaw is an often-served side dish in the Amish home and there are many, many variations. The two recipes that follow are standard for a cold coleslaw and a hot one.

PENNSYLVANIA COLE SLAW

1 head young cabbage
1/2 cup cream
1 tsp. salt
1/2 cup sugar
1/2 cup vinegar

Beat cream, sugar, vinegar and salt together thoroughly until the dressing is like whipped cream. Discard outer leaves of cabbage. Shred the rest finely and combine with dressing just before it is ready to serve. Serves six. As a variation: Add shredded green and red peppers.

HOT SLAW

Shred cabbage finely. Boil in slightly salted water until tender. Drain. Serve hot thoroughly mixed with warm cooked salad dressing made as follows:

1/2 tsp. mustard
1 1/2 tsp. salt
1 1/2 tsp. sugar
1 1/2 Tbl. flour
1/8 tsp. pepper
1 beaten egg
1 cup milk
4 Tbl. vinegar
1 1/2 Tbl. butter

Mix mustard, salt, sugar, flour and pepper. Add egg and mix thoroughly. Add milk and vinegar. Cook over hot water, stirring

[9]Favorite Amish Family Recipes: A Cookbook From Kishacoquillas Valley, (Alymer, Ontario: Pathway Publishing Corporation, 1970), 199.

frequently until thick. Add butter. Cook and stir until melted.[10]

Potato salad of some description is found in nearly every European culture, including that of the Amish. While most of these salads are served cold, the Amish type is served warm.

HOT DUTCH POTATO SALAD

4 slices bacon
1/2 cup chopped onion
1/2 cup chopped green pepper
1/4 cup vinegar
1 tsp. salt
3 hard boiled eggs
1/8 tsp. pepper
1 tsp. sugar
1 egg
1 qt. hot, cubed, cooked potatoes
1/4 cup grated raw carrot

Dice bacon and pan fry. Add chopped onion and green pepper. Cook 3 minutes. Add vinegar, salt, pepper, sugar and beaten egg. Cook slightly. Add cubed potatoes, grated carrot and diced hard-cooked eggs. Blend and serve hot.[11]

Soups are often served at the Amish table, with thick slabs of homemade bread covered with fresh butter and apple butter. The hot, meal warms the tummies of the family and is quick, nutritious fall and winter supper. Always frugal, the Amish housewife has been able to concoct good-tasting soups from just about any ingredients. The basic *rivvel* soup is a great example of making something from almost nothing. It can be eaten as is, or other ingredients, as they were available, were sometimes added.

---

[10]Pennsylvania Dutch Cooking, (York, Pennsylvania: Yorkcraft, Inc., 1960), 21-22.
[11]Pennsylvania Dutch Cooking, 22.

POOR MAN'S RIVVEL SOUP

1 qt. milk
2 Tbl. butter
pinch of black pepper
1 cup flour
1/2 tsp. salt
1 egg, well beaten

Add butter and pepper to the milk and bring to a boil in a two quart saucepan. Combine flour, salt and egg. Rub flour, salt and egg together with the hands until it forms small lumps. Sprinkle these lumps into the boiling milk. Simmer on low heat for five minutes, season with salt and pepper to taste and serve. Serves four.

RICH MAN'S RIVVEL SOUP

4 cups chicken broth
2 cups corn (canned or fresh)
1 cup flour
1/2 tsp. salt
1 egg, well beaten

Bring broth to a boil. Make *rivvels* the same way as in the recipe above and sprinkle the lumps into the boiling broth. Add corn. Simmer 15 minutes. Serves six.[12]

The recipe that follows is a favorite variation of the *rivvel* soup and as long as the corn and chickens last. It is often made in huge quantities for reunions and get-togethers.

CHICKEN CORN SOUP

1 stewing hen, about 4 lbs.
4 qts. water
3 Tbl. flour
10 ears corn
1/2 cup celery, chopped with leaves

---

[12]Emma Byler, <u>Plain and Happy Living: Amish Recipes and Remedies</u>, (Cleveland, Ohio: Goosefoot Acres Press, 1991), 42.

2 hard-boiled eggs
salt and pepper
rivvels

Put cut-up chicken and onion into the water and cook slowly until tender. Add salt. Remove chicken, cut the meat into small (1-inch) pieces and return to broth, together with corn, which has been cut from cob, celery, and seasoning. Continue to simmer. Make *rivvels* by combining 1 cup flour, a pinch salt, 1 egg and a little milk. Mix well with a fork or fingers to form small crumbs. Drop these into the soup, also the chopped hard-boiled eggs. Boil for 15 minutes longer.[13]

Pretzel soup is found in nearly every Amish cookbook and is a simple and filling dish for a busy mother to prepare when swamped with other chores.

PRETZEL SOUP *(SHDREIS'L SUPPEE)*

Mix one and one half tablespoons of butter with one tablespoon of flour. Combine a cup of water and two cups of milk with the flour and butter. Bring the mixture to a boil, adding parsley, pepper and salt. In a large serving dish break a pound of butter pretzels into small pieces, pour the mixture over the pretzels and serve.[14]

Another variation of this soup is to fill a bowl with warm milk for each person. Put a piece of butter in each one and serve. At the table, each person should break up enough large pretzels to fill the bowl.[15]

One-dish main meals are another regular feature in the Amish home and they offer relative ease in preparation and are easily increased to allow enough for the many supper guests who regularly drop in. Pot pies are favorites and can be made with any type of meat. The following recipes are for both

---

[13]Ibid., 4.
[14]The Lancaster County Farm Cookbook, (Lebanon, Pennsylvania: Applied Arts Publishers, 1977), 4.
[15]Pennsylvania Dutch Cookbook, p. 11.

'slippery' pot pie and regular pot pie. The difference is whether the dough is on top of the meat and vegetables or cut up and mixed in with the rest of the dish.

CHICKEN POT PIE *(BOT BOI)*
1 cup flour
1 egg
2 tsp. baking powder
1/2 egg shell of water
small tsp. salt

Mix the above ingredients, roll out and cut in two inch squares. Flour chicken and fry in butter. Put layers of chicken, potato slices, sliced onion and squares of pot pie dough. Barely cover with boiling water and cook for two hours.

BEEF POT PIE
2 lb. stewing beef
6 medium potatoes
pot pie dough
2 onions
chopped parsley
salt and pepper

Cut the beef into 1" cubes, cover with water, season and boil until tender. Peel potatoes, cut into 1/4" slices and slice the onion. Into the hot broth drop layers of potatoes, onions, a sprinkling of parsley and dough squares, alternately, ending with dough on top. Cover and boil for 20 minutes. Stir meat through potpie.

For the pot pie dough:

To two cups of flour, add a little salt, 1 egg, beaten, and enough milk to make a stiff dough. Roll out thin (1/8") on floured board and cut into 2" squares.

Equally good with veal or pork.[16]

Because the Amish are avid hunters and relish the taste of wild game, many of their dishes include a wide variety of game animals and birds.

---

[16]Pennsylvania Dutch Cooking, 10.

SQUIRREL POT PIE

Take one quart of boiling water, one chopped onion, one teaspoon of salt, one teaspoon of butter. Cut squirrel in pieces, flour and fry brown in fat, then add to the liquid mixture and cook one hour.

Make a biscuit dough, cut round. lay it on the potpie and cook until browned. Remove and place the dough on a platter. Thicken the liquid with browned flour in butter and serve.

HASSENPFEFEER

Clean and disjoint a rabbit, bone the meat and place it in a jar, covering it with vinegar. Add an onion sliced and minced, salt and pepper and cloves to flavor and allow ingredients to stand several days. Remove the meat and brown it in a skillet. Pour in the liquid and cook for one hour.[17]

The Old Order Amish have always had to be thrifty and the way they make use of the animals they raise for food attests to that trait. Besides the usual cuts of meat, the Amish find ways to prepare tasty dishes from parts of the animals thrown away by most people!

SOUSE

1 pig's head
6 pigs feet
6 pork hocks
2 teaspoons salt
1/4 tsp. pepper
2 onions, sliced
3 peppercorns
1 bay leaf
1 blade mace
1/4 cup cider vinegar

Clean pig's head, remove tongue and split head open. Clean

---

[17]The Lancaster County Farm Cook Book, p. 15.

pig's feet and hocks. Place pig's head, feet and hocks in a large, heavy kettle and cover with water. Add the salt and pepper. Bring to boiling and cook until tender. Remove meat from liquid and cool. When cooled, remove meat from bones and cut it into pieces. Add sliced onions, peppercorns, bay leaf and mace to liquid in kettle. Boil until liquid is reduced by one-half, strain and cool. Skim fat from cooled liquid. Place fat, meat pieces, in a kettle and bring to boiling. Turn into a crock and add as much of the liquid as it will hold. When cold, this will set and may be cut into slices to fry, or used for salad or sandwich meat.

SCRAPPLE (*PONHAWS*)

Separate hog's head into halves. Remove and discard the eyes and brain. Scrape and thoroughly clean the head. Put into a large heavy kettle and cover with 4 to 5 quarts of cold water. Simmer gently for 2-3 hours, or until the meat falls from the bones. Skim grease from the surface; remove meat, chop fine and return to liquid in kettle. Season with salt and pepper to taste and 1 teaspoon sage. Sift in yellow granulated corn meal, stirring constantly until mixture is thickened to consistency of soft mush. Cook over low heat for one hr., stirring occasionally, as mixture scorches easily. When cooked, pour the scrapple into greased loaf pans and cool. Cover and store in a cool place. To serve, cut into thin slices and fry in hot fat until crisp and browned.

STUFFED BEEF HEART

1 3-3 1/2 lb. beef heart
1 cup cracker crumbs
1 cup roasted chestnuts, coarsely chopped
1/2 cup white sauce
1 tsp. salt

White sauce
2 Tbl. butter
2 Tbl. flour

1/2 tsp. salt

1/8 tsp. pepper

1 cup milk

Melt butter in a saucepan over low heat. Blend in flour, salt and pepper and heat until mixture bubbles, stirring constantly. Remove from heat. Gradually add the milk; cook rapidly until the sauce comes to boiling, stirring constantly. Cook 1 to 2 minutes longer.

Cut arteries, veins and any hard parts from the heart. Wash and set aside to drain. To prepare the stuffing, mix together crumbs and chestnuts. Add whit sauce and mix lightly until thoroughly blended. Stuff heart with the mixture. Fasten with skewers. Place in a Dutch oven: cover heart with water and add salt. Cover and simmer until tender, about 2 hours. Remove heart from water one-half hour before serving and sprinkle with additional cracker crumbs, salt and pepper. Bake at 350 until browned. Carve crosswise into 1/2 inch slices.[18]

HOG MAW

1 pig's stomach

2 lbs. smoked sausage meat, diced

3 cups boiled potatoes, diced

3 cups sliced apples

2 1/2 cups bread crumbs

1 medium onion, chopped

2 cups chopped celery

chopped parsley

salt and pepper

Clean stomach well and soak in salt water. Combine all ingredients and mix well. Stuff the stomach with the mixture and sew up the opening. Simmer for two hours in a large kettle with water to cover. Remove to baking pan with hot fat, brown in hot oven (400) basting frequently. Slice with sharp knife.[19]

[18]Pennsylvania Dutch Cookbook, 24, 29, 40.
[19]Pennsylvania Dutch Cooking, 12.

Although the Old Order Amish are quite well-known for all of their hearty and delicious meals, they are, perhaps, most famous for their desserts. They do love their sweets! The following recipes represent just the tip of the delectable "dessert iceberg" of the Amish culture...

SCHNITZ PIE *(Dried Apples)*

1 lb. of schnitz
1 orange, rind and juice
2 cups sugar
2 Tbl. cinnamon
Already prepared pie crust

Cover schnitz with water and soak overnight. Add orange rind and juice and more water if necessary. Boil until soft and put through colander and add sugar and cinnamon. Pour into pastry-lined shell, dot with butter, cover with top crust or lattice strips. Bake in hot oven (450) for 10 minutes. Reduce to 350 and bake for 30 minutes.

FUNERAL PIE *(RAISIN PIE)*

1 cup seeded raisins, washed
2 cups water
2 1/2 cups sugar
4 Tbl. flour
1 egg, well beaten
Juice of a lemon
2 tsp. grated lemon rind
Pinch of salt

Soak raisins three hours, mix sugar, flour and egg. Then add seasoning, raisins and liquid. Cook over hot water for 15 minutes, stirring occasionally. When the mixture is cool, empty into pie dough-lined pie plate. Cover pie with narrow strips of dough, criss-crossed and bake until browned.[20]

---

[20] Ibid., 39.

SHOOFLY PIE

Dissolve one cup molasses in one cup of water. Mix together four cups of flour, a half cup of butter, three cups of water, and a half cup of lard, a half teaspoon of salt, two cups of sugar, a teaspoon of baking soda and a half cup of cream of tartar. Form mixture into crumbs. Pour the molasses mixture into pie pans lined with crusts. Spread the crumbs evenly on top. Sprinkle with cinnamon and bake in a moderate oven.

FUNNEL CAKES

Combine a pint of milk, two beaten eggs, a pinch of salt, a half teaspoon baking powder and enough flour to make a loose batter.

Place lard in an iron skillet, enough to cover about an inch of dough, heat the lard and then begin pouring the batter through a funnel, beginning in the center of the pan and gradually pouring the dough from the center outward in a circular manner. (Do not allow the dough to tangle the previously poured batter.)

When funnel cakes are a light brown, remove them from the skillet and serve with maple syrup, a tart jelly or simply sprinkle them with powdered sugar.[21]

FASNACHTS (DOUGHNUTS)

This treat is always served on Shrove Tuesday or *Fasnacht* Day in the Amish home. Although they do not always mark the same customs as the "English," this Fat Tuesday corresponds to Mardi Gras in other cultures. The recipes date back to the earliest days of the Amish and have variations. A typical *Fasnacht* recipe follows:

> 5 pounds potato flour
> 3/4 pound granulated sugar
> 3/4 pound lard
> 2 medium eggs
> dash of salt

---

[21]The Lancaster County Cookbook, 18, 27.

3 oz. fresh yeast

6 1/2 oz. fresh cream (just under 1 cup)

13 oz. water at 80 degrees

1. Combine ingredients

2. Mix rapidly for 15 minutes. Dough temperatures should be 80 degrees when completed. Cover and let rise one hour. Knead. Cover and let rise 20 minutes.

3. Roll to 1/4 inch thick and cut into *Fasnachts*. Cover and let rise in warm, humid area for 30 minutes.

4. Fry in 375 degree shortening for 45 seconds on each side, then place on cooling rack. Sprinkle with confectioner's sugar or eat plain.

MOLASSES COOKIES

(These are baked by the hostess for the preaching service to be passed out to the children during the 3-4 hour long session.)

3 3/4 cups shortening

5 cups sugar

11 1/2 cups Bre'r Rabbit molasses

5 eggs

6 tsp. soda

12 1/2 cups sifted flour

1 tsp. cloves

2 1/2 tsp. ginger

2 1/2 tsp. cinnamon

2 1/2 tsp. salt

Melt shortening and cool. Add sugar, molasses and egg. Beat well. Sift together flour, soda, spices, and salt. Add to first mixture. Mix well, chill and form balls. Roll in granulated sugar. Bake in moderate oven 8-10 minutes.

WHOOPIE PIES

4 cups flour
2 cups sugar
2 tsp. soda
1/2 tsp. salt
1 cup cocoa
2 eggs
2 tsp. vanilla
1 cup thick sour milk
1 cup cold water

Cream together: sugar, salt, shortening, vanilla and eggs.

Sift together: flour, soda, and cocoa. Add this to the first mixture alternately with water and sour milk. Add slightly more flour if milk is not thick. Drop by teaspoons. Bake in a hot oven.

WHOOPIE PIE FILLING

2 beaten egg whites
1 tsp. vanilla
2 cups confectioner's sugar

Beat well, add 1 1/2 cups Crisco and continue beating until smooth. Spread this on a cooky (sic). Place another cooky (sic) on top (sandwich style).

This is a very small sample of the fare on the typical Amish table and is, hopefully, enough to whet the appetites of those of us who rely on the warming-up feature of the microwave ovens!

To complete the selection of recipes, the following is one to memorize:

A RECIPE TO LIVE BY

Blend on cup of love and one half cup of kindness, add alternately in small portions one cup of appreciation and three cups of pleasant companionship into which has been sifted three teaspoons of deserving praise.

Flavor with one teaspoon carefully chosen advice. Lightly fold in one cup of cheerfulness to which has been added a pinch of sorrow.

Pour with tender care into small clean hearts and let bake until well matured. Turn out on the surface of society, humbly invoke God's blessing and it will serve all mankind.[22]

---

[22] <u>Favorite Amish Family Recipes: A Cookbook From the Kishacoquillas Valley</u>, 114, 121.

Chapter 10
Transportation

The sight of an Old Order horse and buggy, loaded with kids and their parents, slowly making its way down a country road embodies the image that many "English" folks have of this picturesque lifestyle. The horse and buggy, along with their mode of dress, more than any other facets of their lives, set the Amish apart from the rest of the modern world. They have continued to cling to this outmoded means of transportation long after the automobile has taken over the landscape of the countryside. Although there have been some subtle changes in the styles of horse-drawn vehicles used, they are basically the same as they have been for decades and decades. To the casual observer they are similar, except that some have black tops, some have yellow or brown tops, some have gray tops, some have white tops and some have no tops at all. In reality, there are literally dozens of kinds of buggies, carriages and wagons used by the Old Order Amish in North America.

Although it may seem logical to assume that the Amish have always used horse-drawn vehicles, this is not the case. Among the first documented cases of Amish use of a wheeled vehicle is in 1800, when Christian Zimmerman of the Weaverland area of Lancaster County, Pennsylvania, was given permission to hitch his horse to a wheeled cart. He was a portly man and his weight was too much to allow him to ride horseback. This did not, however, signal an immediate end to the practice, by the Amish, of riding their horses. The Old Order church has always taken to change very slowly and it took nearly a century for the horse-drawn carriage to become the primary mode of transportation. In 1894 David Burkholder, son of deacon Daniel S. Burkholder, was given money to purchase a saddle on his eighteenth birthday. David is said to have refused the gift because now, all the other young people were using buggies.[1] Today, it is rare to see an Amish person astride a horse, as horseback riding is considered to be a worldly pursuit and allows opportunities for pride to take over.

Late in the nineteenth century everybody was getting from place to place via horse and carriage. There was no choice at that time, and so, the Amish were no different from their neighbors. Soon after all of the Amish were using horse-drawn transportation as the norm, a new obstacle came into their lives. In the early 1920's, Henry Ford introduced the automobile to the American people and to the world, and we have not been the same since then. The largely rural society was now able to afford the mode of transportation to take them long distances in a relatively short time and considerably changed the lifestyles of all. As the horseless carriage" became more and more prevalent, the price of one of these machines came down and was within reach of the Amish farmer, the roads were improved and the Old Order Amish began to consider whether they could avail themselves of the opportunity to use the new-fangled mode of transportation. The controversy caused some divisions within the Old Order communities, with some more progressive Amishmen believing that the automobile was a good invention and one that they should be permitted to use. On the other side were the more conservative church leaders who felt that the use of the auto would seriously undermine the basic teachings of the Old Order church leaders. The new mode of transportation would make it easier to travel to faraway towns and cities where the evils of a worldly society were ever present. Because the local church

---

[1]Stephen Scott, <u>Plain Buggies: Amish, Mennonite, and Brethren Horse-Drawn Transportation</u>, (Lancaster, Pennsylvania: Good Books, 1981), 10.

communities were cohesive units by virtue of the fact that traveling great distances was difficult, the leaders feared that their members would lose this sense of community which held them together. The temptation to explore new, forbidden pursuits would be too great for the young people to overcome and the car would be a status symbol, leading to prideful behavior, it was feared. The radio, a forbidden link to the outside world, was present in many autos, and represented another reason for the church leaders to object to their use. One of the primary reasons for its disfavor among the bishops was the requirement for insurance. The Amish carry no insurance, of any kind, and object to their money going to a worldly business. They have a policy of taking care of their needs from within the community and have not found it necessary to rely on the "English" insurance companies. The church leaders formally began to ban the ownership of automobiles by their members in the 1930's and 1940's. Some members persisted in their quest for permission to own them and, eventually, there were new churches formed by these modern-minded persons. The church was very clear on the issue of automobile ownership, but neglected to make a ruling on whether or not it was acceptable to ride in one. During the 1940's and 1950's, as the Amish communities expanded and grew, it became increasingly difficult to visit friends and relatives using the horse and buggy. The bishops were faced with another dilemma, because many Amish families were hiring their "English" neighbors to transport them to social or business functions in distant locales. The Amish "taxis" have grown in popularity and use over the years as more and more Amish are working away from the farm and the home. Today, there are non-Amish people who make a living providing transportation, usually via van, for a price, for the Amish in their community. Some Amish businessmen have hired "English" truck owners to haul their products to markets far from the shop where they are produced.[2] The Old Order leaders have taken a

[2]Donald B. Kraybill, The Puzzles of Amish Life, (Intercourse, Pennsylvania: Good Books, 1990), 44-45.

very strong stand on the automobile. It is **never** to be owned by their members and hired "taxis" are to be used only when necessary and not for frivolous pleasurable pursuits. They have chosen to ignore the young Amishman who is not yet baptized, who keeps a car hidden away for weekend fun. They are ever hopeful that the teachings of childhood will prevail and the young man will make the proper choice and join the church.

To the typical young Amish lad, getting his first buggy is like an "English" boy getting his first car. The girls do not have their own buggies, but are taught, at an early age, to handle the horses, harness them and drive the buggies, pull the plows and do whatever else becomes necessary. Because they are around sixteen and not yet church members, the boys are free to decorate the interiors of the buggies with colorful tape, reflectors and knobs. The seats and walls may be upholstered in fake fur with animal prints or in crushed velvet and the floor may be carpeted. Donald Kraybill has reported the thoughts of one Amish leader concerning the modifications by the youth of his community:

> Some have wall-to-wall carpeting, insulated wooly stuff all around the top, a big dashboard, glove compartment, speedometer, clock, stereo radio, buttons galore, and lights and reflectors all over the place. There's one that even has little lights all the way around the bottom. They even have perfumed things hanging up front, and at Christmas time, some have tinsel and little bells. If they have the money, that's what they do and that's pride. Some of the members even have some of this stuff, but not the radio. These are Cadillacs and some members don't put their Cadillacs away even though they get a little faded.[3]

---

[3]Donald B. Kraybill, <u>The Riddle of Amish Culture</u>, (Baltimore: The Johns Hopkins University Press, 1989), 65.

At one time, especially in Lancaster County, Pennsylvania, the open buggy was the only type permitted for young boys, while the family had a "top buggy" for its travels. The use of the open or "courtship" buggies by young adults is losing favor in most Amish communities and is certainly no longer required. "Boys will be boys," the old expression goes, and this adage is true in the Amish community. Buggy races out in the country among the Amish youth are not unusual and have been going on for years and years. Any "English" teen-ager who has grown up in an area with a large Amish population would have ample opportunity to trade car rides for buggy rides on a weekend evening when the young Amish kids would slip into town for a forbidden movie or trip to the local hang-out. The exchanges often resulted in some racing and daredevil driving as each group showed off for the other. It is a rarity, however, for these events to be staged for public consumption. The following item from a Midwest newspaper illustrates this point very well:

A group of Amish youths defied the rules of their strict religious sect today with plans to stage a "hot rod" buggy race.

From 15 to 20 teen-agers clad in somber buttonless suits of their denomination will race stripped-down buggies at the Elkhart County Fair Saturday for a $350 purse.

To the 500 local members of the stern German sect, that $350 purse means gambling--a thing forbidden to church members.

But the youths said they thought it was time someone broke away from the strict code of the Amish.

"We'll cope with the consequences later," one said.

Goshen residents were surprised at the announcement. Several, however, said they had been expecting something like this to happen.

"These kids are breaking away more and more from the old ways," one said. "We call them `pinkies' or `yanked-over Amish.'"

Amish boys living on farms around Goshen have been racing stripped-down, high-wheeled buggies on the back roads for a long time. But this is the first time they have ever raced in public-- much less for money.

Harness races have been held at the county fair for 30 years, but officials thought they would have to be discontinued this year because of lack of attendance.[4]

The horse-drawn method of getting from place to place has endured in the Amish culture, but has not remained static. The styles and types of buggies and carriages used in the many Old Order communities differ according to church rules and local custom. The bishop and church leaders have the final decision on the details of the buggies. The names of the vehicles also vary from place to place. For example, in Lancaster County, Pennsylvania, the closed in, two seat ones are called carriages and the open, one-seaters are buggies. The spring wagon is an open wagon with heavy-duty springs that is used to haul heavy things, like household furniture and possessions, on the open roads. To get their produce to the market, the Amish use a market wagon, an closed in carriage with a tailgate and a removable rear seat and heavier suspension. The Amish form of "pick-up truck" is a cab wagon. It resembles an open wagon, but has a cab on the front to protect the driver. The two-wheeled cart, with one seat, is also used in some communities by childless couples or retired couples who do not have a family at home to transport. In the midwest the term top buggy or buggy describes the single seat, closed in vehicle and a surrey refers to the closed in, two seat

[4]"Hot Rod Buggy Races," The Goshen News, 24 August 1951, in Amish Roots: A Treasury of History, Wisdom, and Lore, John A. Hostetler, ed., (Baltimore: The Johns Hopkins University Press, 1989), 114-115.

counterpart. Another vehicle with two seats is called a spring wagon or top wagon in the midwest. The open spring wagon, the one with a seat and room to haul things in the back is called a variety of names. In Holmes County, Ohio, it is called a "Hack"; in Arthur, Illinois, a "Buckboard"; in Dover, Delaware, a "Durban"; in Adams County, Indiana, a "Johnny Wagon"; in Daviess County, Indiana, a "Long John"; and in Alymer, Ontario, a "Democrat."[5]

According to Stephen Scott, an expert on the buggy styles of all plain sects, there are four main types of family carriages or buggies. They are named for the state or group in which they predominate:

I. **Pennsylvania Style:** Straight sides. The standard vehicle has two seats with entrance ways to the front seat only. The tops may be black, gray, white or several shades of yellow.

II. **Ohio Style:** Angled-in sides. The standard vehicle has only one seat. The tops are black, only.

III. **Indiana Style:** The top is built around the base of the seat backrest. The standard vehicle has one seat. The tops are black only.

IV. **Swiss Style:** Vehicles with no tops in communities where tops are not allowed. Black only.

Mr. Scott has observed more than 90 variations of the Old Order Amish vehicles.[6] There are apparently many details of the buggy which may be unique to a particular group. The side windows may be of the roll type which are sewn into the canvas of the side flaps of the buggy, or they may be glass and built right into the wooden or canvas sides of the vehicle. Or there may be no side windows at all. The front window, which is called a storm front, a combination of a windshield and a dashboard, may have one or two panes of glass, be removable or permanent and may even be non-existent. The sizes of the buggy windows vary from church district to church district. The rear flap of the

---

[5]Scott, 47.
[6]Ibid., 47, back cover.

buggy may be tacked down, to be unfastened only after a young man marries, or it may be of a roll-up type which can be raised or lowered as weather permits. Some communities favor one or two very small windows, placed high on the back panel of the buggy, and some have no windows, at all, in the back. Some of the buggies have sliding doors, some have doors on hinges or no doors, as such, but a roll-up canvas panel which is raised and lowered as desired. The use of the whip and the whipsocket on the dashboard are items which also vary form group to group. Some of the Old Order bishops have banned the use of the whip because that may lead to a prideful attitude and attempts to show up a fellow Amishman's horse. One thing that is standard on an Old Order Amish vehicle is the use of steel rims around the outside of the wooden wheels. Some vehicles are equipped with brakes, operated by a hand or foot control. Others are now using the more modern hydraulic brake systems activated by a foot pedal. The brake drums are on the front or back wheel hubs. The newer vehicles all come equipped with these more effective brake systems.[7] The use of pneumatic tires, and any other sort of rubber tires, is absolutely forbidden by the more conservative Old Order Amish groups, and that rule prevails in virtually all of those communities.

Even the type of harness and the amount of ornamentation is dictated by the Amish bishops.

The state and federal governments and their laws have often been the basis of controversies throughout the history of the Amish people. The lights on the sides and\or back of the buggies were the source of one of these disputes because of the legal requirements instituted by state governments during the 1920's. The rules of the church did not permit such ostentatious decorations on the buggies, so the leaders were, once again, forced to reach a compromise which would satisfy the legal requirement and, at the same time, maintain the plain appearance of the vehicles. The obvious reason for the lighting legislation was the

---

[7]Ibid., 20-21.

safety of both automobile passengers and those in the buggies. The Amish leaders were aware of this concern and slowly agreed during the 1930's, to permit battery-powered lights for traveling after dark. Although they were opposed to the concept because of its worldly appearance, the use of flashing red lights was allowed, by the 1950's, to comply with the laws. In 1987, there was a slight relaxation of the law by state officials when they allowed the flashing lights to be turned off during daylight hours and used only at night. The next major dispute was over the use of the large reflective triangles to alert other motorists that a slow-moving vehicle was ahead. These symbols were required for farm machinery being taken from field to field by the "English" farmers and the state wanted them on the buggies, which travel at an average speed of 8-10 mph. By the 1970's these triangular signs were accepted and appeared on all Amish vehicles.[8]

A subsequent confrontation with the state authorities came as a result of the increasing numbers of buggies traveling on public roads and the resulting damage to the highways from the steel wheels and horseshoes. Because they had no driver's license and paid no taxes for the upkeep of the roads, there was concern by officials about the large amount of money needed to repair the damage done by the buggies and horses hoofs. In Lancaster County, Pennsylvania, where the controversy began, the officials were aware that the Amish, even in the 1950's and 1960's, were becoming a tourist attraction that would bring revenue to their area. Thus, they wanted to treat the Amish fairly so that they would not leave the area. Once again, a bargain was struck. The Amish would be permitted to travel on public roads, using the steel horseshoes and steel wheels, regardless of the damage they caused, without paying taxes, for road mainte-nance; without having a driver's license and without having to have their vehicles put through an inspection or vehicular licens-ing by the state. They were, however, required to use the electric

---

[8]Kraybill, The Riddle of Amish Culture, 67.

185

lights, flashers, turn signals and reflective triangles, even though these modern additions were quite distasteful to the Old Order leaders. In the end, both sides felt they had a good deal, with the officials believing that the increased income to the area as a result of the tourist industry would offset the dollars spent to repair the roads. The Amish were free to come and go as they wished, and did not have to uproot their families and communities to move to a more secluded area.[9]

In any area where a large number of Old Order communities and church districts exist, one may see several distinctly different buggy styles. As the Amish have migrated to form new communities, some changes have been made. Sometimes the reason for the relocation is to seek a more liberal church which allows for modifications in the vehicle styles. The newly formed settlements may well have members from several different church communities and it takes some time for the new styles to emerge and be adapted to the new rules. But, just as the garb of the Old Order Amish people sets them apart and allows the astute observer to identify which church community they are affiliated with, the buggy style, similarly, reveals the church group of its driver.

Purchasing a new family buggy is not quite the same as loading the kids in the old clunker and heading down to the local car dealership to trade it in. First of all, there are not a lot of "dealers" to choose from and the models are basically all the same within a church community. Also, buggies are not traded in on a newer model, as they are driven until they can no longer be repaired or restored for use. The typical buggy can last for a period of several decades if it is taken care of and most families only own the buggies they absolutely must have to get their families from place to place. The cost of a new buggy is reported to be anywhere from $350.00 for a two-wheeled cart to $2450.00 for a one seat top buggy and a buggy can take as long as one month to be built.[10] Some of the buggy shops make all but the

[9]Ibid., 67.
[10]Scott, 22, 25.

wheels of a vehicle and some are more specialized. The business of repairing the buggies is one that is also necessary and provides a source of income for some Amish craftsmen. Simple repairs are usually done by the owner of the carriage, but more complex jobs are done by a "specialist," just as we "English" may change the oil in our automobile, but need to take it to a skilled mechanic to replace the sophisticated computer chips in today's engines.

Combined with the Amish buggy, the driving horse is the major component of the Old Order Amish transportation in and around the local community. The average Amish farmer owns at least two driving horses along with his one or more teams of draft horses or mules. The two are never used interchangeably. The driving horses used by the Amish are "retired" harness racing horses or ones that have not passed muster on the racing circuit. These Standard Bred animals are either trotters or pacers in the racing world, depending upon the style of harness racing event they compete in. A trotter's opposite front and rear feet are off the ground at the same time, e.g. if the right front foot is off the ground, then the left rear will also be raised. A pacer's feet move in unison on one side or the other, e.g., if the front right foot is off the ground, then the right rear foot will also be raised. The gait of a pacer is a bit faster than that of a trotter. Some Amishmen travel directly to a racetrack to purchase a new buggy horse, but most of the time they find the steed they need at local horse sales. The Amishman can expect to pay anywhere from $450.00-$2300.00 for a driving horse at auction, depending on age, condition, bloodlines and a large number of variables known by those who deal in horseflesh. A horse's disposition is very important and finding a suitable one may be difficult. Speed is not the only consideration. The horse must be able to heed commands in traffic, not balk and get nervous at railroad tracks and in heavy traffic. Too much spirit in a driving horse can pose a real danger. The horse must be fitted with horseshoes so travel on paved roads will not harm its feet. These shoes are removed periodically so that the hooves can be trimmed and rasped or filed, just like human nails. The shoes have a lifespan of 6-7 months, depending on how much travel is done and on what type of road surface. The horses are well cared for and receive visits from the veterinarian if needed. The are well-fed and are given daily vitamins. The average, healthy driving horse can serve a family for as long as fifteen years. Their speed is 8-10 mph and a horse can travel 20 miles or so without a rest.

The obvious link between the horse and the carriage is the harness. This is another product produced by specialists within the Amish community. The harness is almost always made of leather, although there some ares where newer nylon material is permitted for harnesses. The fit of the harness is important and there must be no rough places to rub the horse and cause sores. The cost of a new harness varies with community, but in Lancaster County, Pennsylvania, a person can expect to pay $55.00 for a horse collar and $235.00 for the leather harness and collar together. At auctions used harness may bring as little as $40.00 or as much as $170.00. The average life of the harness is really not possible to determine, but the following excerpt from a horse training manual includes a cautionary note:

> Does anyone know how long a driving harness will last? I don't and I don't want to find out. I would rather sell my harness or give it away when 3/4 worn out than to use it on a colt until it breaks. This could ruin a colt. I once knew a man who had poor hold backs, and incidently, they finished wearing out as he was going down a hill. The horse, not being thoroughly broken, kicked and ran away and he had a real smash up. A couple of his children were taken to the hospital and doctor bills and buying a new buggy and harness could have bought him a barrel-full of the best hold backs available and he would have had money left over.[11]

[11]Owen Brumbaugh, <u>Training the Buggy Horse and Training the Driver</u>, (Bradford, Ohio, By the author, 9585 Yount Rd., 1981), 32.

The driving harness is somewhat different from the harness used on the draft horses. For one thing, the driving horses are never used in pairs and the draft horses are rarely used singly. Also, the very great size difference makes interchanging the harness impossible.

Learning to put the harness correctly on the horse is just one of the skills learned by both Amish boys and girls. The driving, itself, requires great strength, knowledge of horsemanship and courage. All too frequently the headlines tell of a mishap involving an Amish vehicle and a truck or automobile. The Amish are very much aware that they have an obligation to be responsible for their own safety and to that end, have tried to reach large numbers of their population with a reminder of their duty through their publications. One such article is reprinted here:

Are you a Considerate Driver?

Common courtesy on the road can save lives, and very possibly your own. Why is it that it sometimes appears that we as plain people think it is a sign of weakness to be considerate of others on the road?

Although it is never really very safe to drive along busy highways with horse-drawn vehicles, fortunately, there are ways to reduce the danger. Such vehicles should travel as far on the shoulder of the road as possible and if there is room to drive beside the hard surface, so much the better. If it is necessary to travel in the lane of traffic then those who follow should leave a space between each vehicle long enough for a car to get into at all times. It's a lot easier to pass only one or two buggies than a long string of them. If you drove a car and were in a hurry, how would you feel? Not hard to imagine, is it?

If you think you own half the road and insist on

taking up one whole side of the road, then remember who makes the laws and that in most states it is against the law for a slow moving vehicle to hold up the traffic needlessly. If you think you have a right to the road because you pay tax, consider that a large portion of the upkeep expenses for the roads comes from the gasoline tax. A horse does not use much gasoline.

It is our Christian duty to try to keep up the goodwill of those we meet on the road. If we fail to do so, we are neglecting our duty.

Have you ever seen the wave of the hand and the smiles of the motorist after you have given him the all-clear signal when he couldn't quite see over the hill yet? I have and it feels a lot better than to hear the sound of the roaring motor and slipping tires as the exasperated motorist finally pulls around you after having to poke along behind you for some time. This gives you a guilty feeling because you know you have angered someone by sloppy driving, by being rude and inconsiderate.

But just a word of caution, be sure the road is clear before you give the signal to pass.[12]

The horse, buggy and passengers are all at risk when they are out on a crowded highway, competing with speeding, impatient motorists for a place on the road. The antics have ranged from throwing objects at the Amish vehicles and shouting derisive remarks to bumping into the rear of the buggies with cars. The added hazard of harassment by "English" young people makes it difficult to remain separate and away from the public eye. One tragedy resulted when something was thrown into a buggy by boys in a pick-up truck. The incident is recounted below by Simon M. Schwartz:

---

[12]Anonymous, "Are You a Considerate Driver?," Family Life, January, 1976, in Plain Buggies: Amish, Mennonite, and Brethren Horse-Drawn Transportation, Stephen Scott, (Lancaster, Pennsylvania: Good Books, 1981), 17.

It was Friday night, August 31, 1979, the close of a hot, humid day in Indiana.

The air was still stifling as Levi and Rebecca Schwartz and their seven children headed back to their farm in their black horse-drawn buggy. The Old Order Amish family had spent the early evening visiting friends near Berne, Indiana. Already thirsty, the children talked longingly of the lemonade they had been served.

The clacking of the horse's hoofs and the creaking of leather as they headed north on the Adams county road spoke of the simple life of the Plain People. It was a hard life, but uncomplicated. Because of their strict religious beliefs they had no automobiles or tractors. Their house was heated by coal- and wood-burning stoves; kerosene lamps reflected the shining cleanness of the wood floors and rustic furniture. The children, ranging from Adeline, seven months, to Margaret, eleven, would go through the eighth grade and then take their places in the closely knit Amish community of 2,000 living in Adams County.

The bed would look good after another long, hot day, Levi remarked to his wife. Even the brown horse pulling the buggy seemed to agree, quickening its pace as they got within three miles of the hundred acres Levi farmed. Traffic was heavy, with shoppers from Berne slowing as they saw the triangle-shaped red safety reflector Indiana requires on Amish buggies. The Schwartzes waved as they recognized occupants.

At 9:30 P.M., as nearly as the Schwartzes can remember, a battered old pickup pulled alongside. As it passed, Mrs. Schwartz, who was holding Adeline in her arms, felt a sharp pain in her right wrist. "Somebody threw something from that pickup," she said. A quick check of the children revealed no injury, and the Schwartzes continued home.

The modest but well-kept farmhouse was only a white blob in the darkness when the family arrived. As Levi waited patiently to take the horse to the barn, Rebecca handed Adeline to Margaret. "Take her into the house and put her on the bed while I get the others in," she directed.

As Margaret turned up the wick on the kerosene lamp, she noticed blood on the baby's face. Running outside, she cried, "Mother! Mother! Come quick! Something's wrong with Adeline!"

Levi and Rebecca ran into the house, and the mother anxiously picked up the infant. Immediately they saw a large bump on the back of Adeline's head. Blood was spattered on her face, which looked strangely pale and peaceful in the lamplight. Perhaps she's only unconscious, Mrs. Schwartz found herself hoping, as she wiped the blood from the baby's face. But she could detect no breath.

"She's dead! She's dead!" she cried in anguish. Quickly the dazed father ran to the nearest neighbor who had a telephone. "Call the Emergency Medical Service and the police," he begged. "Adeline may be dead."

She was. A piece of clay tile thrown from the truck had fractured Adeline's skull. She probably died instantly while still in her mother's arms.

Soon city, county, and state police cars were systematically covering town and country roads in search for the battered pickup. Earlier in the evening police had been notified that youths in such a vehicle had been throwing objects at Amish homes and buggies.

An hour after the tragedy, the truck was spotted in nearby Berne and the four young occupants were taken into custody, handcuffed, and driven to the Adams County jail in Decatur, twelve miles to the north. There, charges of reckless homicide were filed against the four. Two of the youths, seventeen and eighteen, were from Berne; the others, eighteen and nineteen, were from Monroe, five miles to the south. Within a week, families of the four had posted $10,000.00 bond and the four were released pending trial.

From the first, the reaction of the youths was one of shock and remorse. "We had no idea we had injured, let alone killed, someone," they said. "We were just out for a little fun."

As the news of the tragedy made headlines across the nation, hundreds of letters and sympathy cards arrived at the Schwartz's farm. Others, addressed to the police, mayors and newspapers in Berne and Decatur, demanded quick justice for the four youths.

Locals, too, were stunned and horrified by the senseless tragedy. But there was also concern and compassion for the youths and their families, all of good reputation in the community. None of the young men had been in trouble before, and all were popular among their acquaintances. Still, so incensed was public opinion that they had to go outside the county to find attorneys to defend them.

The four had pleaded not guilty when arraigned and had asked for jury trials. But when three were tried ten months later, in Adams Circuit Court, they changed their pleas and threw themselves on the mercy of the court.

Before sentencing the three, Judge Herman Busse, of Fort Wayne, Indiana, ordered a month-long investigation to help determine their sentence. Even in their communities, odds were in favor of their having to serve some time.

On July 29, 1980, Judge Busse sentenced the first two defendants, announcing his verdict to the crowded courtroom. He knew that no sentence, however harsh, could return Adeline to her mother's arms. But the crime could not go unpunished. Each youth was given a five-year prison term, but Judge Busse suspended the sentences, put the youths on five years' probation, fined them $5,000.00 and court costs and ordered them to make full restitution to the Schwartz family for medical and funeral expenses. In September, Judge Robert Thompson gave the third youth three years' probation and a $5,000.00 fine.

The sentences might have been much harsher had it not been for a plea entered in the youths' behalf by the bishop of the Amish community. His letter, endorsed by the Schwartzes, was read in court.

"We believe," he wrote, "that the four boys have suffered, and suffered heavily since the crime, and that they have paid for what they did Sending the defendants to prison would serve no good purpose, and we plead for leniency for them."

This remarkable expression of compassion by the Amish community, many of whom had been harassed by the defendants and others, brought tears to the eyes of onlookers in the courtroom and gained additional friends for the Plain People.

Today, Amish buggies around Berne and Monroe seldom draw more than a cheery wave from passing vehicles. Levi and Rebecca Schwartz like to think that each wave is a tribute to baby Adeline. If so, her death was not in vain.[13]

Horse-drawn transportation has endured as a symbol of the separateness of the Amish and their dedication to a simple, unworldly lifestyle. The slowness of horse and buggy travel allows plenty of time for thinking and contemplation and provides a restful break from the toil of everyday life in an Amish home. Amish children, like children in every culture, seem to have a way of putting the basics into perspective, as this poem written by a young woman illustrates:

A Buggy Ride

Who'd want to drive a motorcar
    When he could have a horse?
There may be many others who
    Would take a car, of course.
They do not know the joy of it,
    A horse and buggy ride.
The feel of wind upon your face.
    No stuffy seat inside.
Along the road we hear the birds sing,
    And watch a squirrel dash,
And just enjoy the scenery
    Instead of rushing past.
The sound of horses' trotting feet
    Is music to the ear.
No car is ever half as nice
    At any time of year.

[13]Simon M. Schwartz, "Baby Adeline," in Amish Roots: A Treasury of History, Wisdom, and Lore, John A. Hostetler, ed., (Baltimore: The Johns Hopkins University Press, 1989), 252-255.

True, the winter's snows are very cold
And rain makes me quite wet.
The wind can be uncomfortable--
Our fingers freeze, and yet,
I still would choose a buggy ride,
In spite of cold or heat.
I shall insist that it is true,
A buggy can't be beat.

Rhoda, age 16 [14]

Because visiting far away family and friends is such an important part of the Amish culture, there have been concessions made by the bishops to allow for more efficient travel to those places. In addition to the liberty to use hired "taxis" for trips that are too long for Horse and buggy travel, the church leaders have granted permission for their members to travel via public transportation. This is largely limited to trains, trolleys and commercial bus lines, however, and air travel is not condoned. The only time they might be permitted to fly is in the case of an emergency or a death and special permission must be given in advance. The feeling is that the airplane is not really necessary in ordinary circumstances because the trains and buses can take people anywhere in North America. If an Amish person must travel across an ocean, then air travel is permitted, but ground transportation must be used upon arrival in the foreign country. The airplane poses a threat to the unique sense of community within the Amish society and is entirely too worldly to even be considered as a regular means of transportation. In addition, the bus and train offer no opportunity for any increase in status within the community as the airplane could.

On a smaller scale, there are forms of self-propelled transportation that have caused a small stir within the church leaders. Namely, the two-wheeled bicycle is a tempting way for Amish young people to get around, but the bishops are well aware of the possibility that great distances could be covered in a relatively

[14]Joe Wittmer, The Gentle People: Personal Reflections of Amish Life, (Minneapolis, Minnesota: Educational Media Corporation, 1991), 2-3.

short time and there would be a loss of control if two-wheelers were allowed. The young people could easily ride off at will and blend more easily into the world at large on a bicycle. They could hide a bicycle a lot more easily than they could hide a horse and buggy and, perhaps, deny their heritage for a short period of freedom. The small children are permitted to use tricycles and toy wagons, as they are obviously not in a position to defy authority and go off into the worldly sunset. A seeming enigma in the Amish community is the widespread use of scooters. They seem, at first, similar enough to the two-wheeler that "English" observers would expect them to be banned, as well. However, they are not nearly as fast or as efficient as the bike and the permission to ride them represents another one of the compromises the church leaders have reached. The irony is that rubber tires are not permitted on farm machinery, tractors or buggies and, yet, the bicycle, some scooters and some wheelbarrows have pneumatic tires and are allowed to be used. The leaders apparently feel that the agreement allows them to maintain control of the means of transportation that affords the Amish person easy access to the temptations of the world far away from their church community. Other types of "transportation" used frequently by the Amish young people are roller skates and the currently popular rollerblades or in-line skates. These are used extensively and seem to pose no real threat to the continuity of the Amish lifestyle. Snowmobiles and all-terrain vehicles are not permitted under any circumstances because the clearly have no purpose but for recreation and speed just for the sake of speed. This is totally outside the realm of entertainment permitted by the Old Order Amish church.

CHAPTER 11
AMISH FUNERALS

The Old Order Amish person lives in such a way that death is the culmination of a long journey, the reward for years of prayer and adherence to the Scriptures. Their strong belief in life everlasting is a source of comfort to the bereaved family and community. The Amish attach great importance to the dignity of death and prefer to die in their homes, surrounded by those dearest to them, if at all possible. Because such importance is attached to visiting the sick, there is a steady stream of callers at the home of the one who is ill. The callers simply enter and take their turn for a short time at the bedside of the ailing one. When death is imminent, the extended family gathers to comfort one another and to spend some final hours with the dying individual. All of the visiting is done quietly and is quite somber. The person closest to the dying person is greeted by those who sit in the main room of the home waiting for updates on the condition of the patient. When the death does occur the undertaker is notified by a family member or friend who will go to an "English" neighbor's house to use the telephone. The laws of most states require embalming and that is the main responsibility of the undertaker when someone from an Amish community passes away. The issuing of burial certificates is the only other task of the funeral director. The news of the death is soon spread and by the time the undertaker arrives to remove the body, there is usually a group of friends already there, to see the deceased just as he or she was at the end and to offer comfort and solace to the family.

Some of those present have begun to organize the preparations for the next several days. The burial is normally three days after death and if it happens during "wedding season," the priority is for the wedding, and the funeral is scheduled accordingly. The body is taken to the funeral home just long enough to be embalmed and is returned to the home as quickly as possible to be prepared for burial. The friends make all arrangements, from construction of the coffin to dressing the body. The six pallbearers are chosen from among the relatives and the grave is dug. The viewing of the body is done in the home and the preaching service and eulogy are also done in the home. As one would expect, the funeral and the customs surrounding a death are simple and straighforward, with no showy displays of flowers or elaborate ceremonies. Every person is given the same kind of funeral service, somber and dignified, and there is no difference in status in death, as in life, in the Amish community.

The coffin is a simple one and is made by members of the community. It is a simple pine box, much like the ones used a century ago, with six sides which are angled to slightly widen near the top third of the box. Depending on the local custom, the lid may be one piece or may be in two sections, with the division about one third of the way down. This allows the lower portion to be closed while leaving the upper area of the body and head available for viewing by the mourners. In some communities the face of the deceased is covered by a crisp white linen cloth and removed by a church member when mourners file past the coffin. Some communities line the coffin with a white material while others do not. The coffin is taken to the undertaker who dresses the body in undergarments and places it in the coffin after the embalming is completed. If the death was unexpected and sudden, the body may simply be laid out on a wide board suspended between two straight chairs and covered with a white sheet until the coffin is built. The body is returned to the home and the women dress it, all in white. The men are dressed in a white shirt, trousers and socks. The women are dressed in a white cape, dress, apron and cap, usually the ones she wore on her wedding day. Shoes are not put on the bodies.

Meanwhile, the grave at a nearby Amish cemetery is being dug by several relatives of the deceased who have had the honor of being chosen for the task. The wooden vault is also being made by members of the community. There is little expense for an Amish funeral beyond the embalming fee and the nominal cost of the coffin. The funeral service is plain and simple, without flowers, artificial grass and mechanical lowering equipment at the gravesite, limousines and a hearse for transportation or a tent for the committal service.

At the home where the funeral will take place, an older couple will have taken over all of the household duties and will oversee the cleaning, cooking and other preparation for the service and the meal following the burial. A group of young men will take over the chores from the time of the death until two or three days following the funeral. This frees the family of the deceased of all worry and responsibility as they endure the loss of their loved one. Other young men called leicht-ah-sager will travel throughout the community issuing invitations to the funeral service. All members of the church community are automatically invited, but relatives from other church districts are issued invitations. Funerals are often attended by several hundred friends and relatives. When the body is ready for viewing it is placed in a room away from the main rooms of the house. In most Amish communities a kerosene lantern is left burning on a table near the body at all times. The family sits quietly in the living room and receives the guests who pay their respects and express their sympathy with a handshake after viewing the body. The guests remain in the living room with the family and friends, sitting quietly and offering comfort to the bereaved. The women of the immediate family will be dressed in black as soon as the death occurs and will continue to wear black throughout the mourning period. The traditional mourning period is one year for a member of the immediate family, six months for a grandparent, three months for an aunt or an uncle and six weeks for a cousin.

The funeral service is much like the preaching service, starting early in the morning and lasting for several hours. The body is then taken to the cemetery and mourners are permitted to view it just before burial. Following the funeral, the friends and family members return to the home for a meal and fellowship which is designed to help the family to return to their normal routines as soon as possible.

The grave will be marked with an unadorned headstone on which the name of the deceased will be noted, along with birth and death dates, in years, months and days. The headstones are all identical in an Amish cemetery. The funeral will be reported in The Budget, and other local newspapers that carry Amish news.

A very poignant description of the funeral of an Amishman from Mifflin County, Pennsylvania is offered by John A. Hostetler and is printed below.

> On our arrival the barnyard was already full of black carriages. People were gathering slowly and silently in the large white house, first removing their overshoes on the long porch. Inside there were three long rooms. The wall partitions had been removed so that the speaker could be seen from any part of the three rooms. Benches were arranged parallel with the length of each room. About three hundred people were present. The living room held sixty-two persons, including fourteen ministers (many of them guests) seated on a row of chairs down the center of the room. The large kitchen seated probably eighty persons and the third room held about fifty persons, including children. Of the remaining people, some were upstairs, others were standing in the summer kitchen, and more were outside. The third room ordinarily the master bedroom, has been used as

the living quarters of the deceased grandfather. It was in this room that the body of the deceased was resting—in a coffin that had been placed on a bench against the wall. Relatives sat facing the coffin, with the next of kin closest to it. They had their backs to the speaker.

The house gradually filled. The head usher was a friend of the family but not a close relative. With a hat on his head, he seated incoming people and reserved special space for relatives. When every bit of available bench space was full, and the chairs had been crowded in at all possible odd corners, the worshippers waited in silence for the appointed hour.

After the clocks in all three rooms struck nine the minister at the head of a long line of preachers removed his hat. At once all the other men removed their hats in perfect unison. The first minister took his place at the doorway between the kitchen and the living room. His message, similar to an ordinary introductory sermon at a regular worship service, was full of Biblical admonitions, largely from the Old Testament. The gathering, he reminded his hearers, was special. God had spoken through the death of a brother.

He made reference to the life and character of the deceased, but these remarks were incidental to the sermon, which continued: "The Departed brother was especially minded to attend worship services the last few year of his life, in spite of his physical handicaps. Those who ministered to his needs have nothing to regret because they have done their work well. His chair is empty, his bed is empty, his voice will not be heard anymore. He was needed in our presence, but God needs such men too. He would not wish him back, but we should rather prepare to follow after him. He was a human being and had weaknesses, too, but his deeds will now speak louder than when he lived."

After thirty minutes the first speaker sat down. He was followed by a second minister, a guest in the community, who delivered the principal address. He too reminded his hearers that a cloud call had come to the congregation and that the Scriptures warn every member to be ready to meet death. "We do not know when 'our time' will come, but the important thing is to be ready," the minister warned. "Death is the result of Adam's sin. Young people, when you are old enough think about joining the church, don't put it off." (Such direct admonitions to the young, linked with intense emotional appeal, provide motivation for conformity to traditional Amish values.)

Two passages were read, one near the beginning and one near the close of this second address. The readings were from John 5 and Revelation 20. The sermon was far from a eulogy. The emphasis was personal and direct. It was an appeal for the audience to love righteously, inasmuch as a day of reckoning comes for all people. The minister did not wish to make the sermon too long because the weather was unpleasant for the horses standing outside in the rain. After speaking for forty-five minutes, he read a long prayer as the congregation knelt. At the conclusion of the prayer the audience rose to their feet and the benediction was pronounced.

At this point the audience was seated and a brief obituary was read in German by the minister who had preached the first sermon. In behalf of the family he also thanked all those who had shown kindness during the sickness and death of the departed one and invited all who could to return to the home for dinner after the burial. The assisting minister read a hymn. There was no singing.

The minister in charge announced that the boys could retire to the barn. The reason was apparent, as rearrangement was necessary to provide for the viewing of the body. Except for the ministers, the living room was entirely vacated. Next, the coffin was moved to a convenient viewing place in the main entrance. Everyone present formed a line and took one last look at the body of the departed brother. Sorrow and tears were evident, but there was little weeping. The closest relatives stood in back of the coffin during the viewing and followed it to the grave.

Meanwhile friends and helpers had prepared the hearse for transporting the body to the *Graabhof* ("graveyard.") The hearse consisted of the one-horse spring wagon with the seat pushed forward. Because of the rainy weather, a canvas was placed over the coffin to keep it dry. The horses of the mourners were hitched to their carriages by the many helpers. Relatives of the deceased entered their carriages and formed a long line to follow the body to the graveyard. The procession traveled very slowly, seldom faster than the ordinary walk of the horses.

Upon arrival at the graveyard the horses were tied to the hitching posts. The coffin, supported by two stout, rounded hickory poles, was immediately carried to the open grave and placed over it. Relatives and friends gathered near. Long, felt straps were placed around each end of the coffin.

The pallbearers lifted the coffin with the straps while a bystander quickly removed the supporting crosspieces. The coffin was then slowly lowered into the grave and the long straps were slowly removed. Standing in the grave on the frame that surrounded the casket, a man placed short boards on the casket as they were handed to him. Nearby a father clutched his four-year-old son and whispered something into his ears, hoping that some recollection of his grandfather would remain in his consciousness. With shovels the four pallbearers began to fill the grave. Soil and gravel hit the rough box with loud thumps. When the grave was half filled the shovelers halted as the minister read a hymn. As is their custom, all the men tilted or removed their hats. They filled the grave and mounded the soil. Family members turned from the scene, slowly got into their buggies, and returned to the home of the deceased to share a meal together.[1]

There are a number of superstitions surrounding death among the Amish. Some of them have been collected by A. Monroe Aurand, Jr., and are included here.

Omens that foretell a death:

> If cracks appear in bread as it bakes; if a dog whines beneath a window; if a cricket gets into the house; if a row is missed when planting; if the buggies are counted in a funeral procession or if anyone in the procession looks back; or if a tombstone is erected less than a year after a burial, another will occur in the family soon. ...if the eyes of a corpse are open they are looking for the next one to follow, and if thirteen sit down to a meal one of them will die soon.

[1]John A. Hostelter, <u>Amish Society</u>, (Baltimore: The Johns Hopkins University Press, 1993), 204-206.

Other admonitions concerning death:

> The windows should be opened in the death chamber immediately after the death so that the soul can get out. Always wash a new shirt before it is worn, because if you are taken sick in an unwashed one, you will never get well. Move the bee hives when the funeral is over to prevent the bees from dying or becoming worthless.[2]

Other death-related superstitions garnered from conversations with the Amish are that if it rains in an open grave or if the body lays over a Sunday there will be another death in the family very soon. To ease the broken heart that results from losing a loved one, visit the grave and bring a few stones from it home in your pocket. You will not miss that person as much.

The Old Order Amish conduct their lives so that they will be assured a place with the Lord on Judgment Day. Because of the strict adherence to the Scriptures, death is not a dreaded event, but, rather is considered the logical conclusion of such a life. The family and friends of the departed will, of course, miss that person, but they take solace in the belief that they are surely with God and will be joined by the living when they, too, receive their Heavenly reward.

---

[2]A. Monroe Aurand, Jr., Popular Home Remedies and Superstitions of the Pennsylvania Germans, (Harrisburg, Pennsylvania: The Aurand Press, 1941), 29-30.

Chapter 12
Epilogue

The Old Order Amish have endured for more than three centuries, despite persecution, oppression and mistreatment that seem too horrendous to believe and forces from all areas of society that would seem to undermine their very existence. They live in relative harmony with the rest of the modern world which moves at a pace far more hectic and faster than theirs. One of the greatest threats to their way of life is the tourism industry. Admittedly, the tourists bring some prosperity to the Amish, themselves, but they would do without the extra income if they could go back to being the private, separate people they want to be. In 1972, Britain's Lord Snowdon visited the Amish communities in Lancaster County, Pennsylvania. His observations of twenty years ago have a message for today's people.

> Visiting the Amish community is like visiting a very large agricultural rural monastery...

> But nothing had prepared me for the exploitation I would find of these peaceful, enormously hard-working people. And most of all, I never imagined I would come away so deeply moved nor so emotionally involved with and affected by their way of life...

> Fourteen years ago, some Lancaster businessmen formed the Pennsylvania Dutch Tourist Bureau to advertise and promote the region. And

since then, the serene Amish country has become pockmarked with some sixty motels, with restaurants, amusement parks, museums, service stations and countless gift shops selling such souvenirs as Amish dolls made in Hong Kong.

While the tourist board has tried hard to romanticize and cash in upon the Amish, the attitude of the Amish people (who rigorously shun publicity) and the philosophy which governs life remains every bit as obscure as before. During my own stay, for example, I encountered maps and brochures of the Amishland at every turn, but I could find no literature about their religious beliefs. It is almost as if no one is expected to take them seriously in terms of what they believe but rather only in terms of what they look like...

"Now with this tourist business," an Amish farmer said to me, "well, we feel sometimes it's getting monotonous. But we hope and pray that it won't get too much worse. I figure if I go about my business and they let me alone, I'll let them alone. I feel that if it's wrong, God will give them their punishment, not me."

"We want to be the kind of Christians that the world can see are different. We believe you're supposed to lead a life so that anyone can see you're a Christian, so that you don't have to carry the Bible under your arm."

It is so ironic and tragic that the Amish, who originally settled here on the basis of William Penn's offer of religious liberty, should ultimately be forced to seek their liberty elsewhere. But, speaking as an outsider, I believe that hope still exists for keeping them together and on their own land. I can't compare the Amish with anything I know in Europe; they are a uniquely American phenomenon...

There is no way of preventing people from staring at things that fascinate them. But when the object of their attention is another group of human beings, it would seem to me necessary to "go the second mile"—to approach them not only better informed about their world, but with a sense of honest reverence, the kind of common courtesy and respect for privacy that people normally display towards others.[1]

To echo Lord Snowdon, the purpose of this work is to provide an opportunity for looking beyond the quaintness and cuteness of the Amish people. The idyllic lifestyle touted in the tourist industry's brochures is a simplistic way of observing these amazing people who have defied the odds and continue to thrive. They lose fewer that 20% of their young people to the evil world they contend with on a daily basis and their population continues to double every 20 years or so. They face more backbreaking toil in a day than many of us will see in a lifetime and, yet, they are sincerely committed to their religion and their rigorous lifestyle. They have endured torture at the hands of others, technological challenges that would test the most tenacious among us and strife within their ranks. They are now faced with a whole new group of technological temptations...and it will be most interesting to watch them keep pace with the "traffic" on the information highway as they make their way in horses and buggies. The twenty-first century may be the greatest challenge that they have ever had to face...and, face it, they will. It is this writer's belief that, knowing them as I do, the Old Order Amish will persevere well beyond the next century.

---

[1]Lord Snowdon, "The Plight of the Amish...," McCall's (April 1972); 88, 124-125, in John A Hostetler, ed., Amish Roots: A Treasury of History, Wisdom, and Lore, Baltimore: The Johns Hopkins University Press, 1989, 282-283.

BIBLIOGRAPHY

Amish Church of Pike County, Ohio. "*Ordnung* of a Christian Church." Pike County, Ohio; Privately printed, 1950.

Amish Favorite Recipes: A Cookbook From Kishacoquillas Valley. Alymer, Ontario: Pathway Publishing Corporation, 1970.

Aurand, A. Monroe, Jr. Little Known Facts About Bundling in the New World. Lancaster, Pennsylvania: The Aurand Press, n.d.

Popular Home Remedies and Superstitions of the Pennsylvania Germans. Harrisburg, Pennsylvania: The Aurand Press, 1941.

Brandt, Mindy and Thomas E. Gallagher. "Tourism and the Old Order Amish." Pennsylvania Folklife 42 (Winter 1992-93): 71-73.

Brumbaugh, Owen. Training the Buggy Horse and Training the Driver. Bradford, Ohio: By the author, 9585 Yount Road, 1981.

Byler, Emma. Plain and Happy Living: Amish Recipes and Remedies. Cleveland: Goosefoot Acres Press, 1991.

Denlinger, A. Martha. Real People: Amish and Mennonites in Lancaster County, Pennsylvania. Fourth Edition. Scottsdale, Pennsylvania: Herald Press, 1993.

Ensminger, Robert F. "A Search For the Origin of the Pennsylvania Barn." Pennsylvania Folklife 30 (Winter 1980-81): 50-70.

Hershberger, Alma. Amish Women. Danville, Ohio: Art of Amish Taste, 1992.

Holliday, Albert E. "The Amish and Compulsory Education." Pennsylvania Education 3 (January-February 1972): 6-10.

Hostetler, John A., ed. Amish Roots: A Treasury of History, Wisdom, and Lore. Baltimore: The Johns Hopkins University Press, 1989.

Hostetler, John A. Amish Society. Fourth Edition. Baltimore: The Johns Hopkins University Press, 1993.

Amish Society. Third Edition. Baltimore: The Johns Hopkins University Press, 1980.

Amish Society. Second Edition. Baltimore: The Johns Hopkins University Press, 1968.

Hutchison, Bernadette. "Amish Gardens: A Symbol of Identity." Pennsylvania Folklife 43 (Spring

1994): 136-139.

Korson, George, ed. Pennsylvania Songs and Legends. Philadelphia: The University of Pennsylvania Press, 1949.

Kraybill, Donald B. The Puzzles of Amish Life. Intercourse, Pennsylvania: Good Book, 1990.

The Riddle of Amish Culture. Baltimore: The Johns Hopkins University Press, 1989.

The Lancaster County Farm Cookbook. Lebanon, Pennsylvania: Applied Arts Publishers, 1977.

Lehman's Non-Electric Catalog. Kidron, Ohio: n.p. 1994.
Lestz, Gerald S. Amish Culture and Society. Ephrata, Pennsylvania: Science Press, 1984.

Lustig, Lillie S., ed. Pennsylvania Dutch Cookbook of Fine Old Recipes. Reading, Pennsylvania: Culinary Arts Press, 1967.

McClearn, Norma Fischer. A History of the Amish People and Their Faith. New Wilmington, Pennsylvania: New Horizons Publishing Company, 1994.

Meyer, Carolyn. Amish People: Plain Living In a Complex Society. New York: Atheneum, 1976.

Miller, Ruth. The Bulk Food Cookbook/The Amish of Our Time Described in Rhyme. Sugarcreek, Ohio: Schlabach Printers, n.d.

Nolt, Steven M. A History of the Amish. Intercourse, Pennsylvania Good Books, 1992.

Patton, Gayle. "Plain and Simple Pleasures: Bookmobile Service In Amish Country." Wilson Library Bulletin (March 1994) 31-33, 139.

Pellman, Rachel and Kenneth. The World of Amish Quilts. Intercourse, Pennsylvania: Good Books, 1984.

Pennsylvania Dutch Cooking. York, Pennsylvania: Yorkcraft, Inc., 1960.

Schreiber, William I. Our Amish Neighbors. Wooster, Ohio: The College of Wooster, 1962.

Scott, Stephen. Amish Houses and Barns. Intercourse, Pennsylvania: Good Books, 1992.

Plain Buggies: Amish, Mennonite, and Brethren Horse-drawn Transportation. Lancaster, Pennsylvania: Good Books, 1981.

Seguy, Jean. "Religion and Agricultural Success: The Vocational Life of the French Anabaptists From the Seventeenth Through Nineteenth Centuries." Mennonite Quarterly Review 47 (July 1973), 182.

Wittmer, Joe. The Gentle People: Personal Reflections of Amish Life. Minneapolis, Minnesota: Educational Media Corporation, 1991.

Yoder, Joseph W. Rosanna of the Amish. Scottsdale, Pennsylvania: Herald Press, 1973.